PSYCHEDELIC
ADULT COLORING BOOK

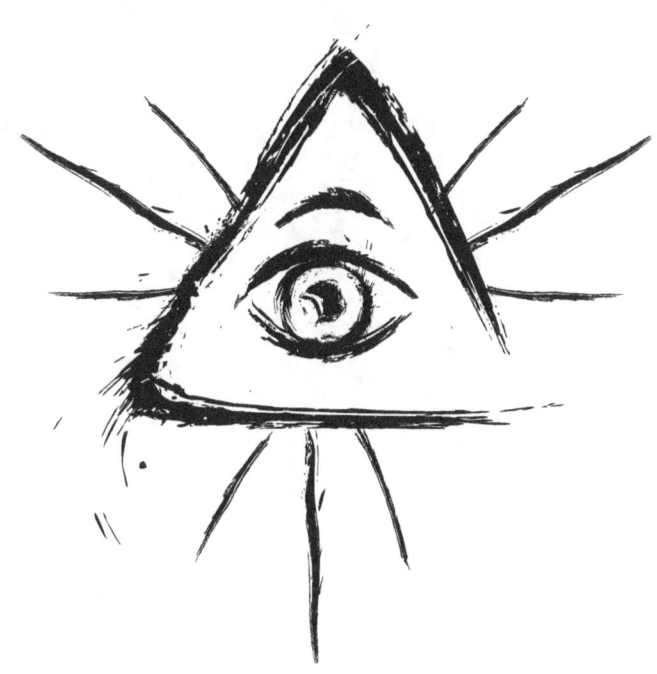

Loelli Publishing

The content contained within this book may not be reproduced,
duplicated, or transmitted without direct written permission from
the artist, author, or the publisher.

ISBN - 9798695303650

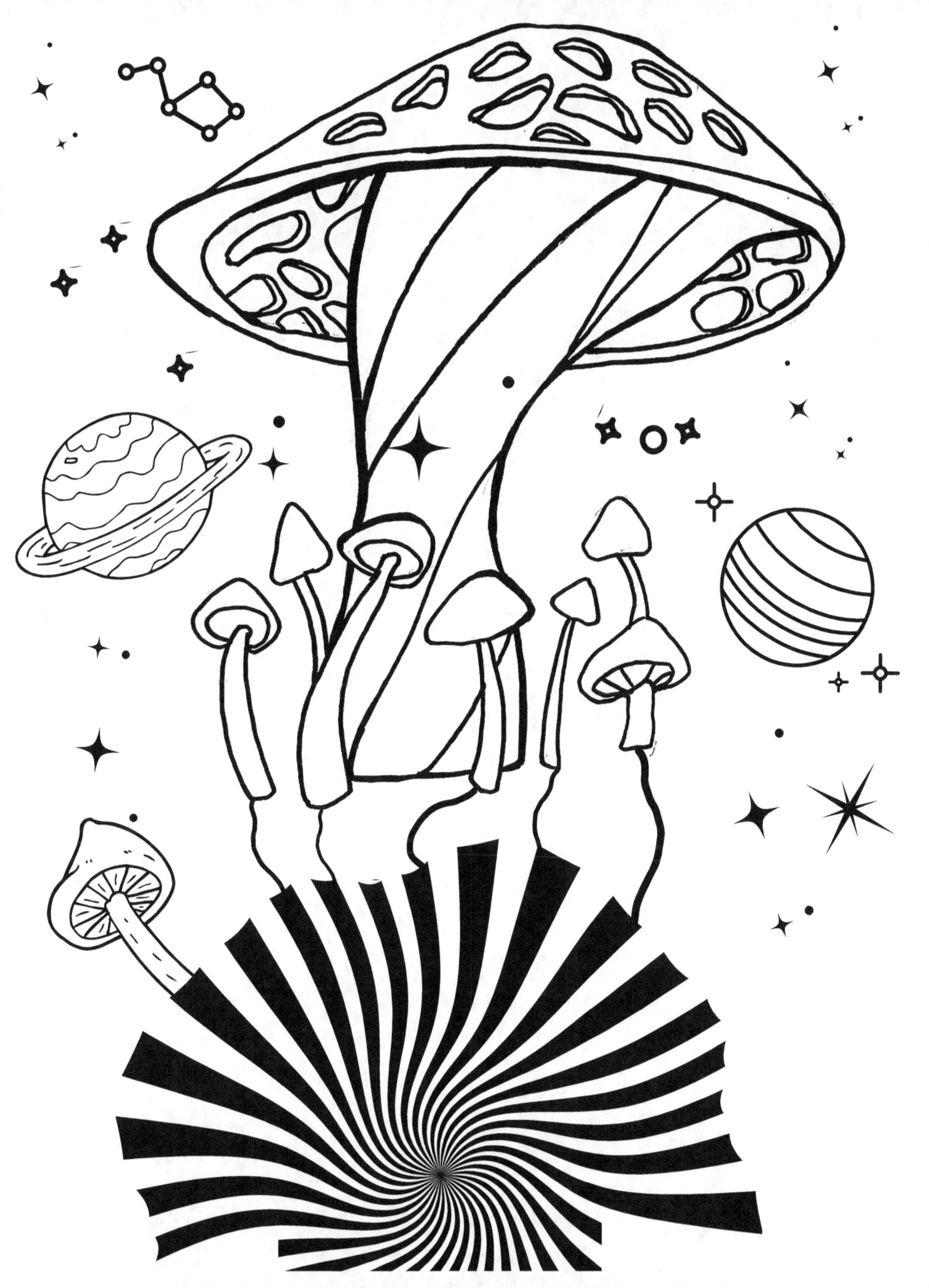

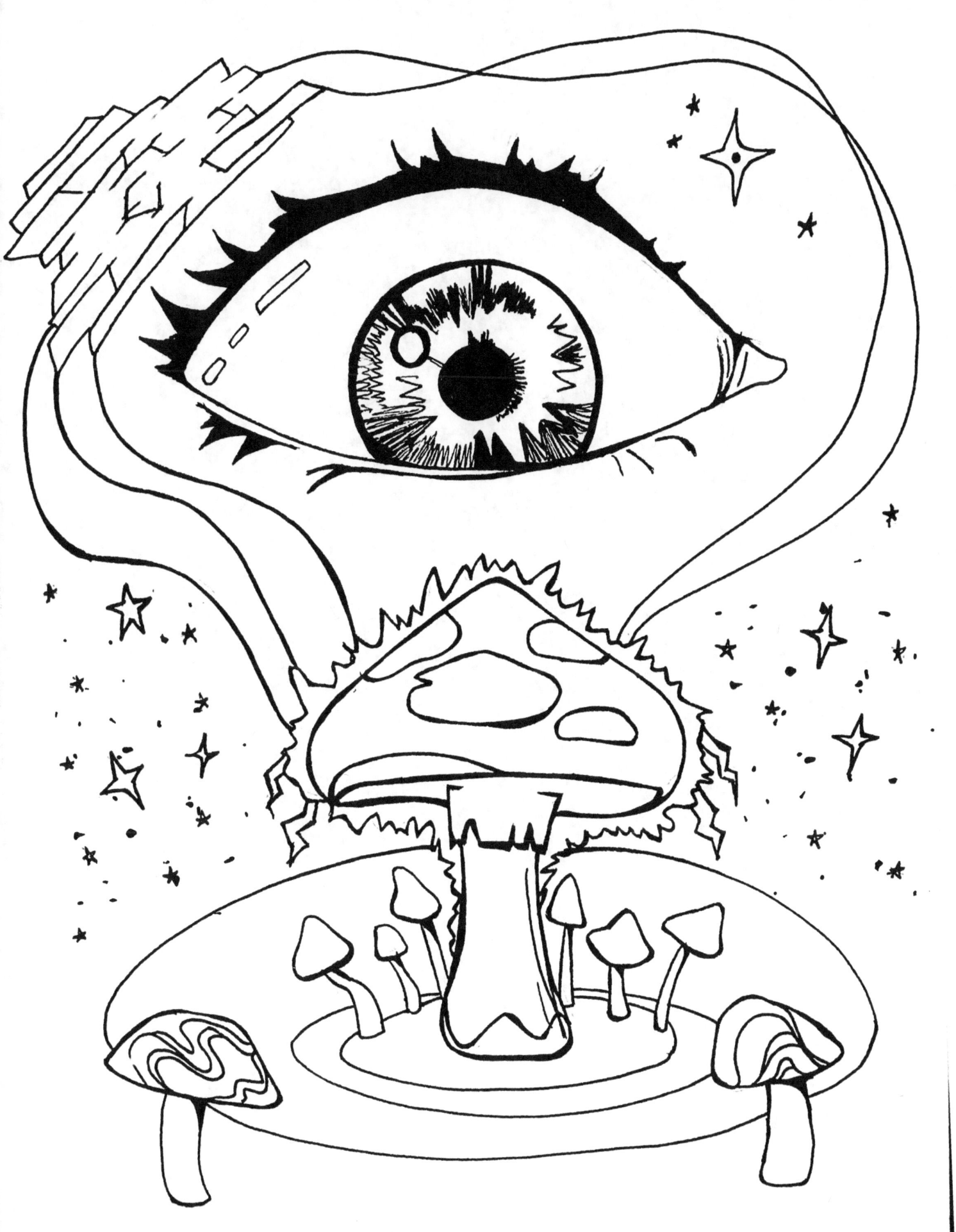

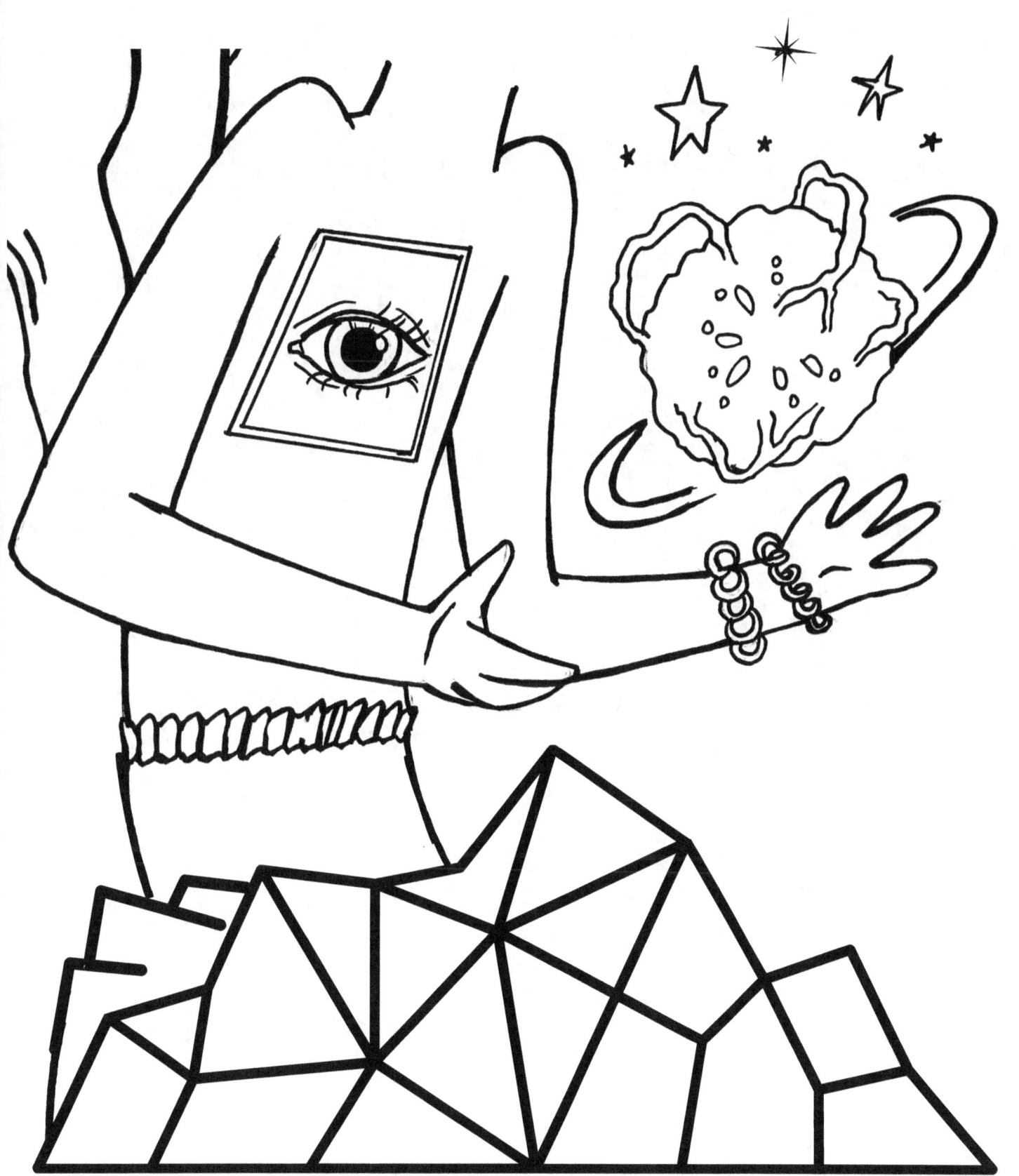

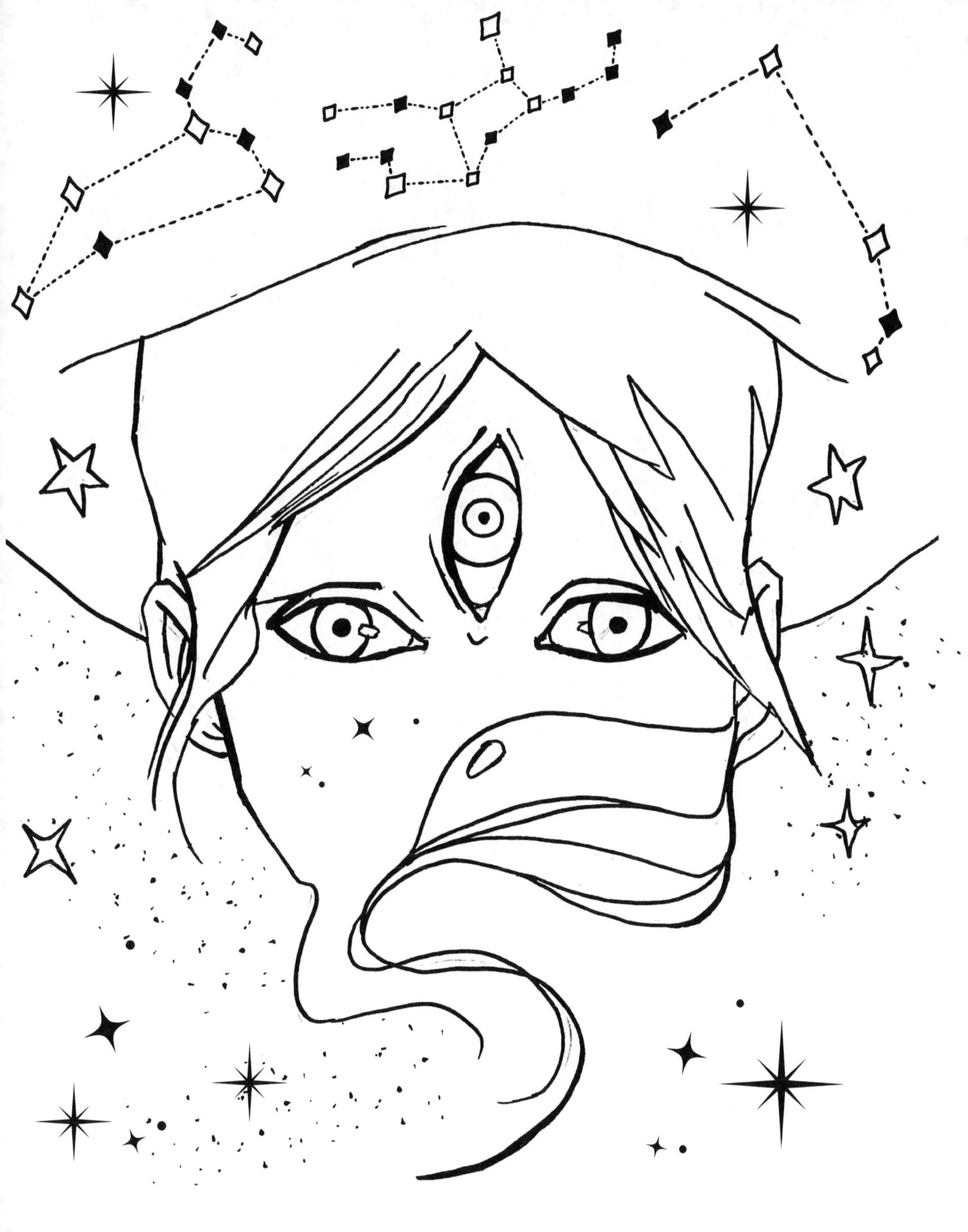

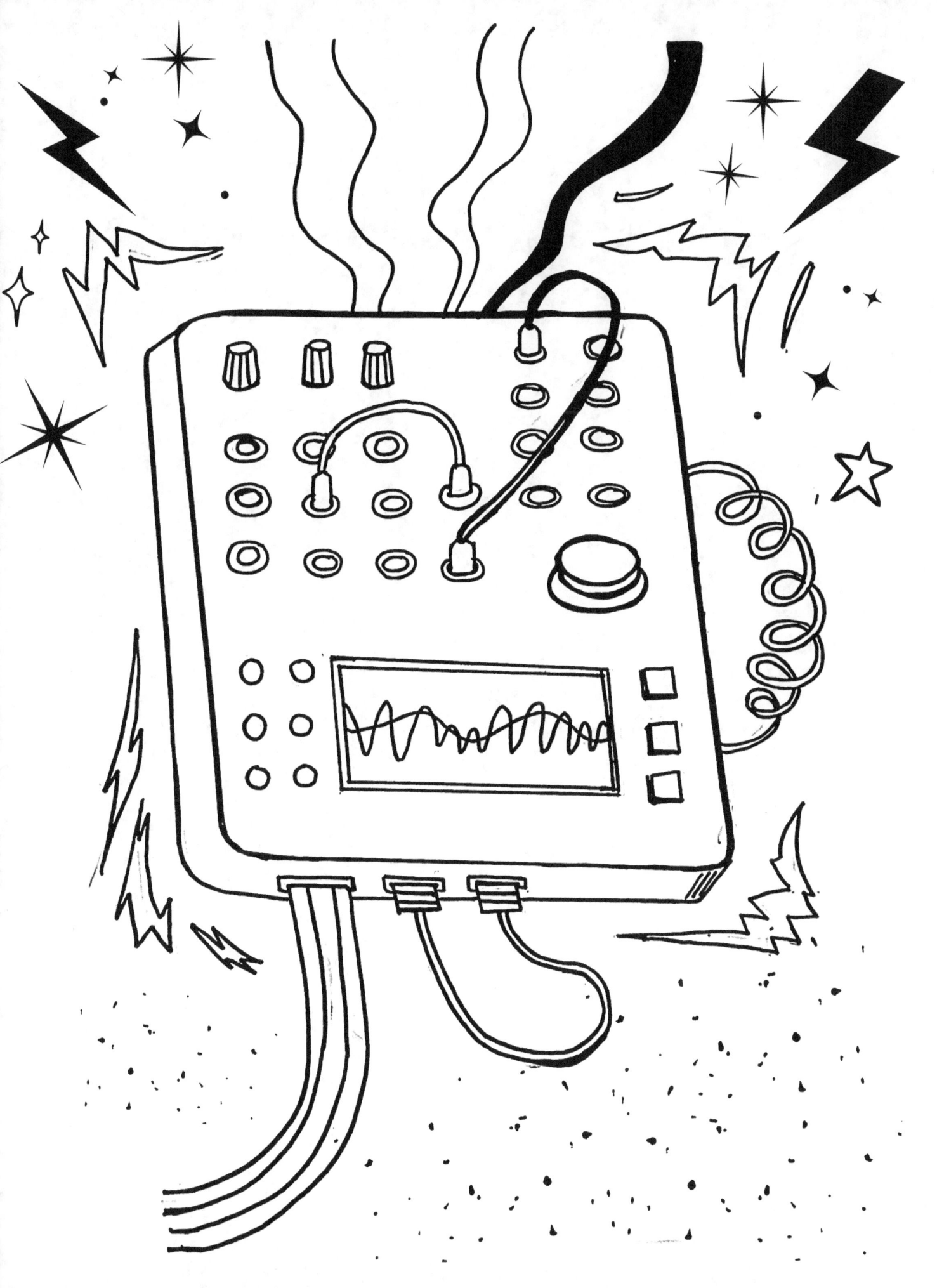

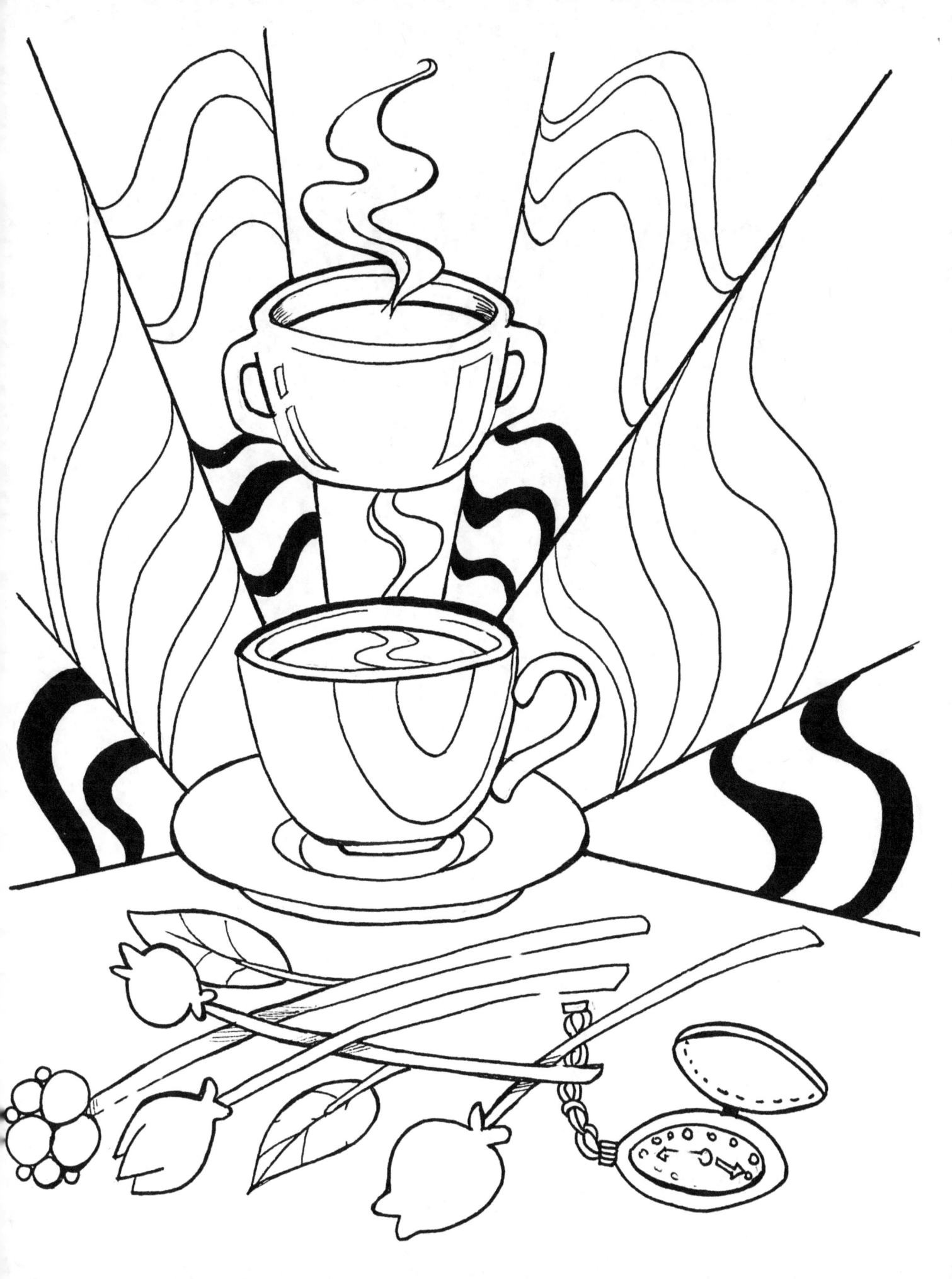

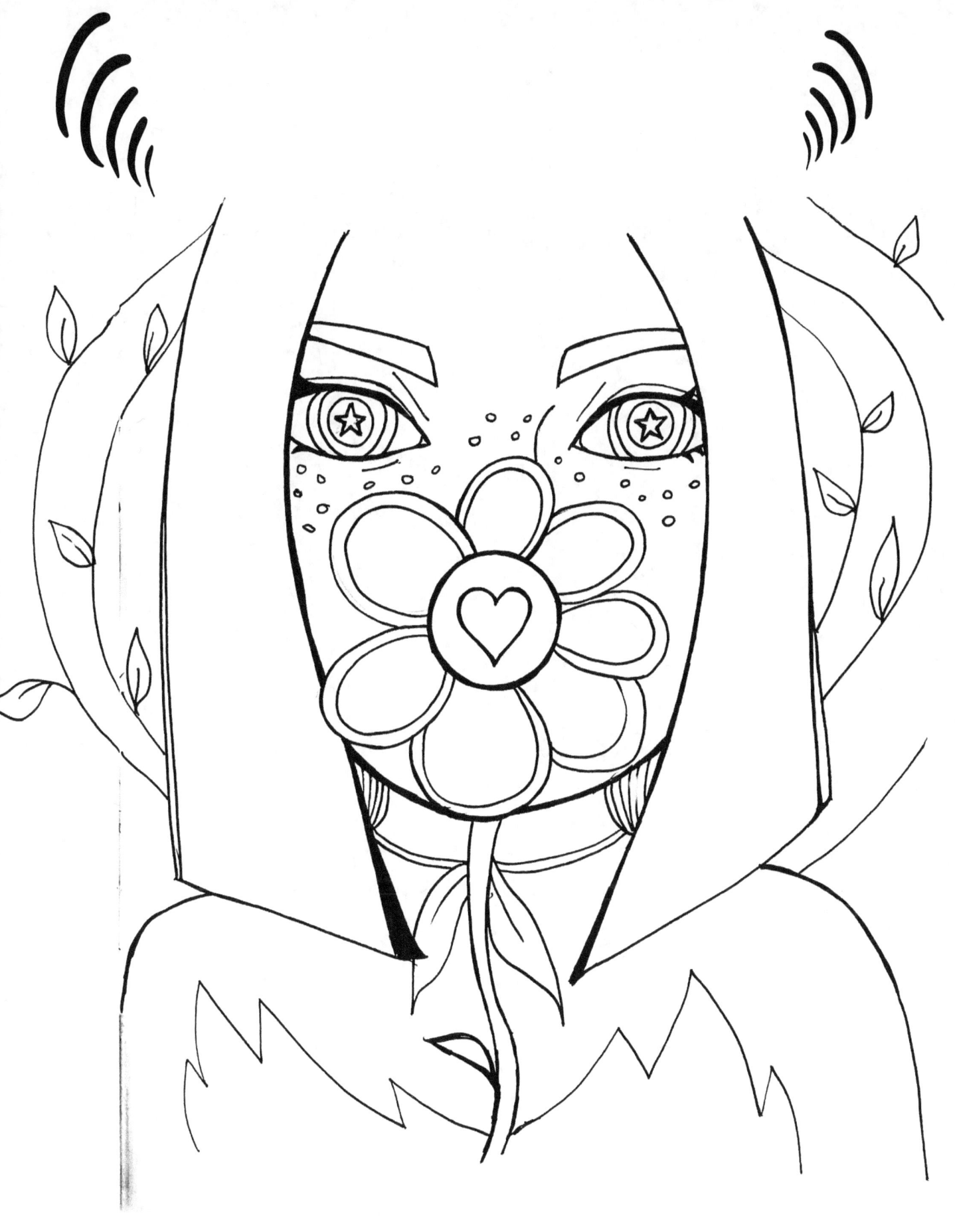

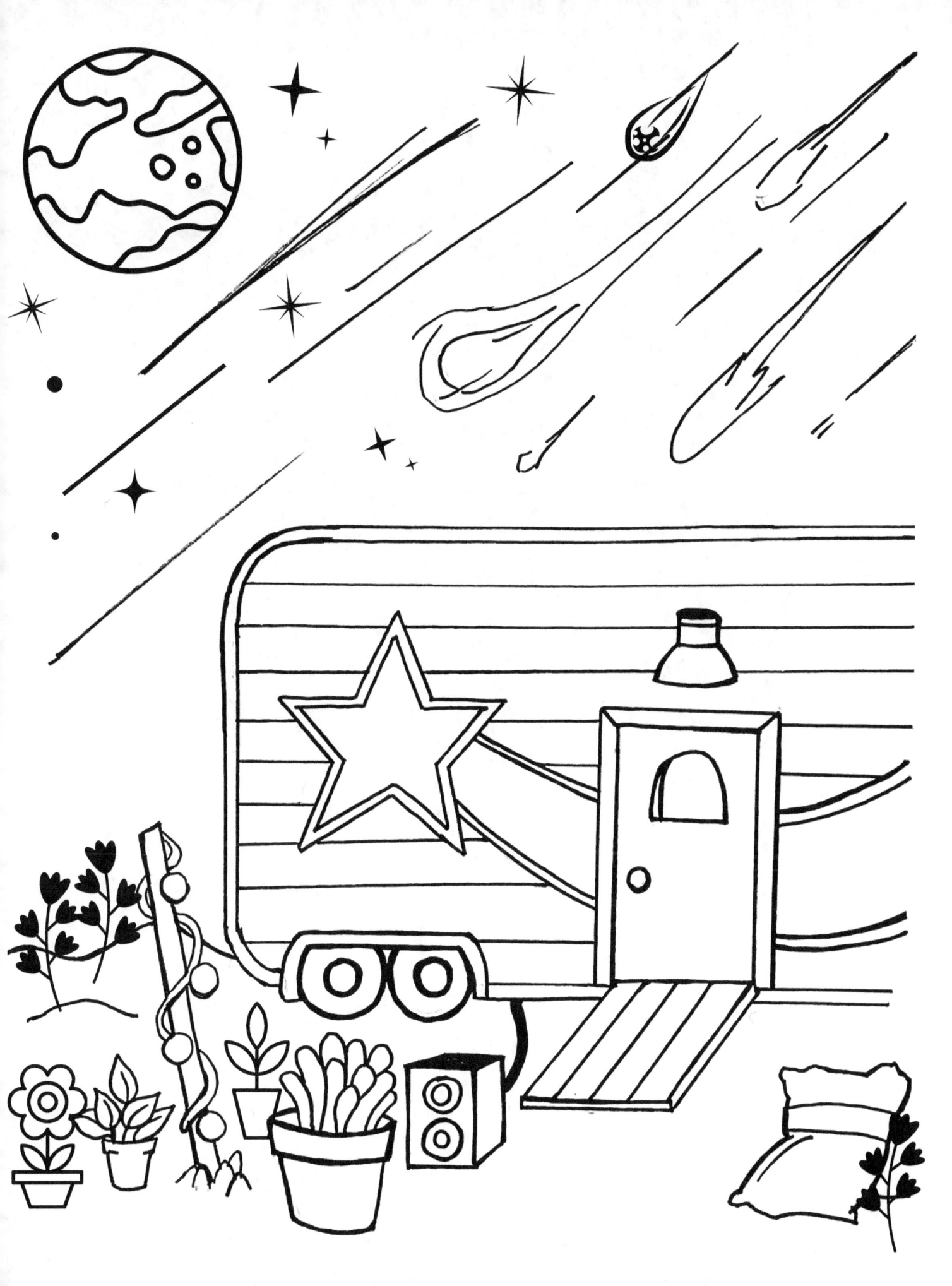

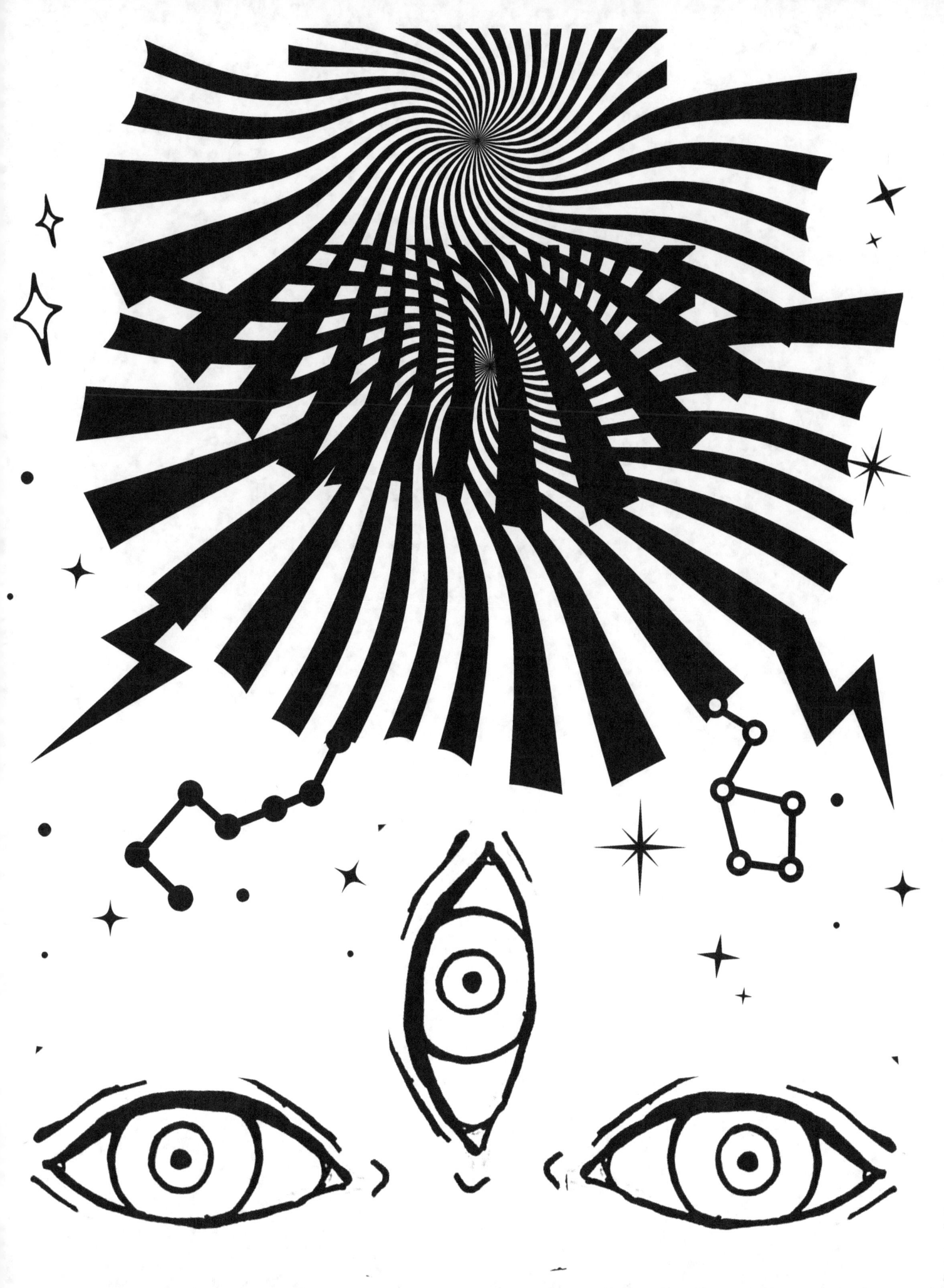

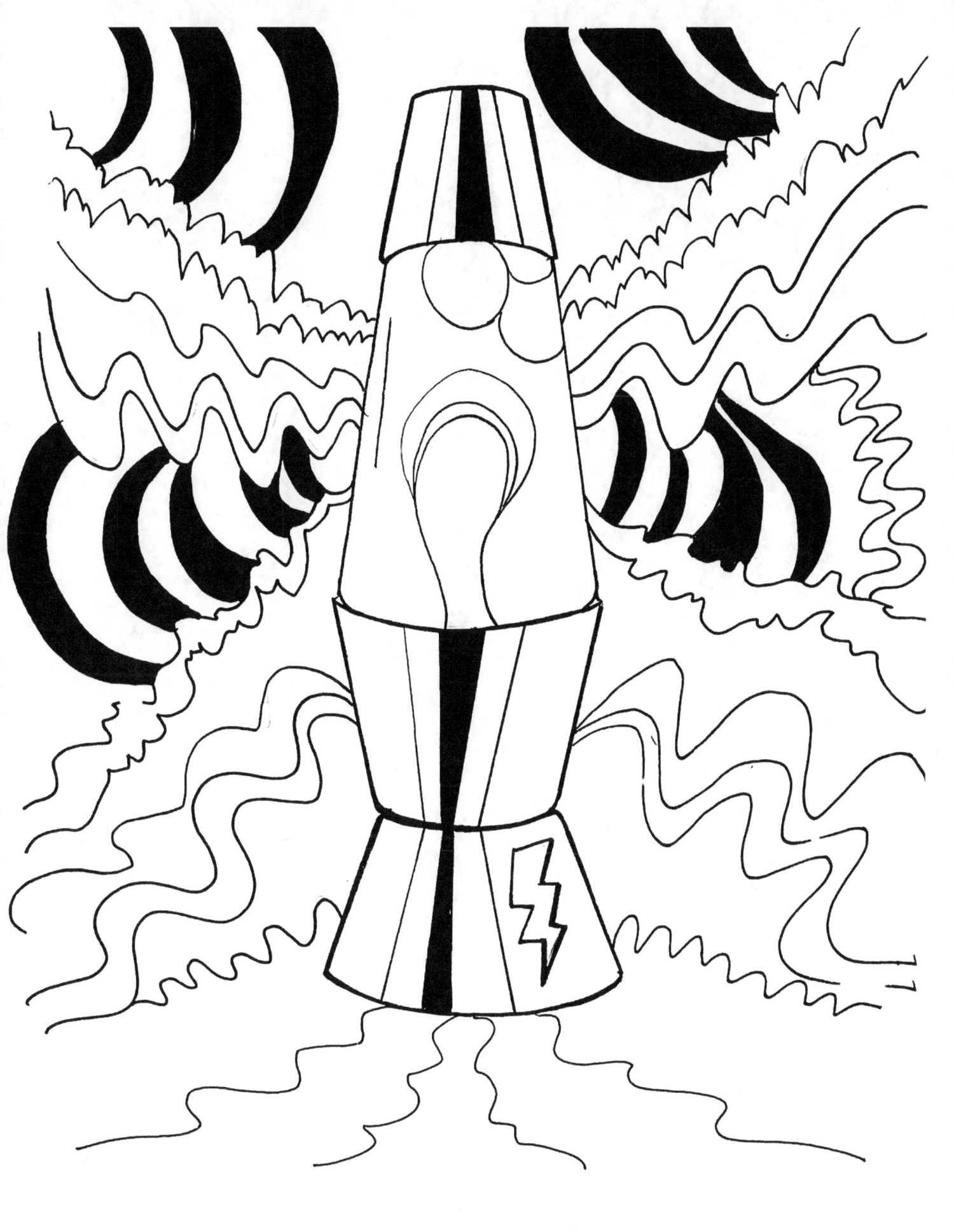

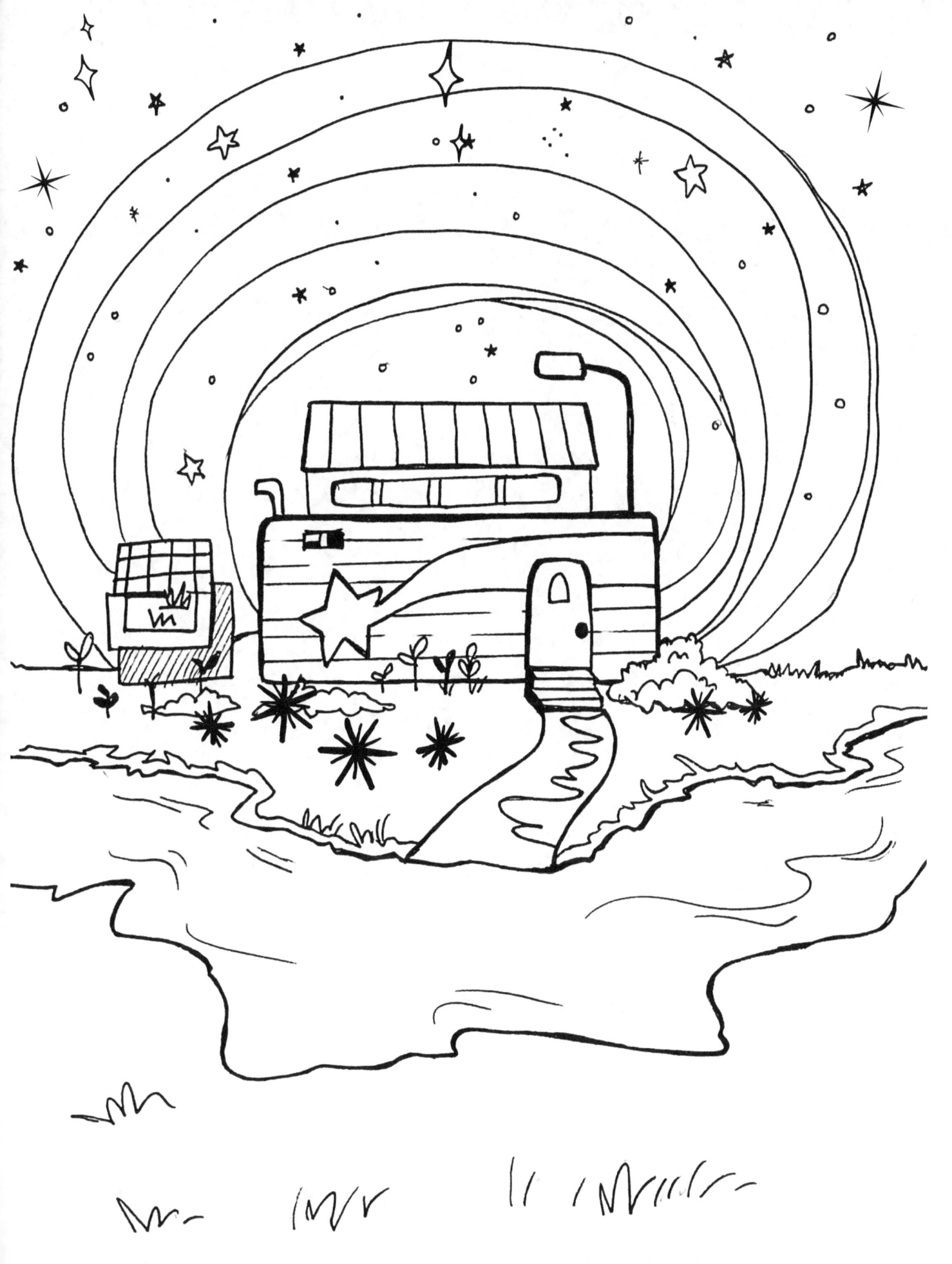

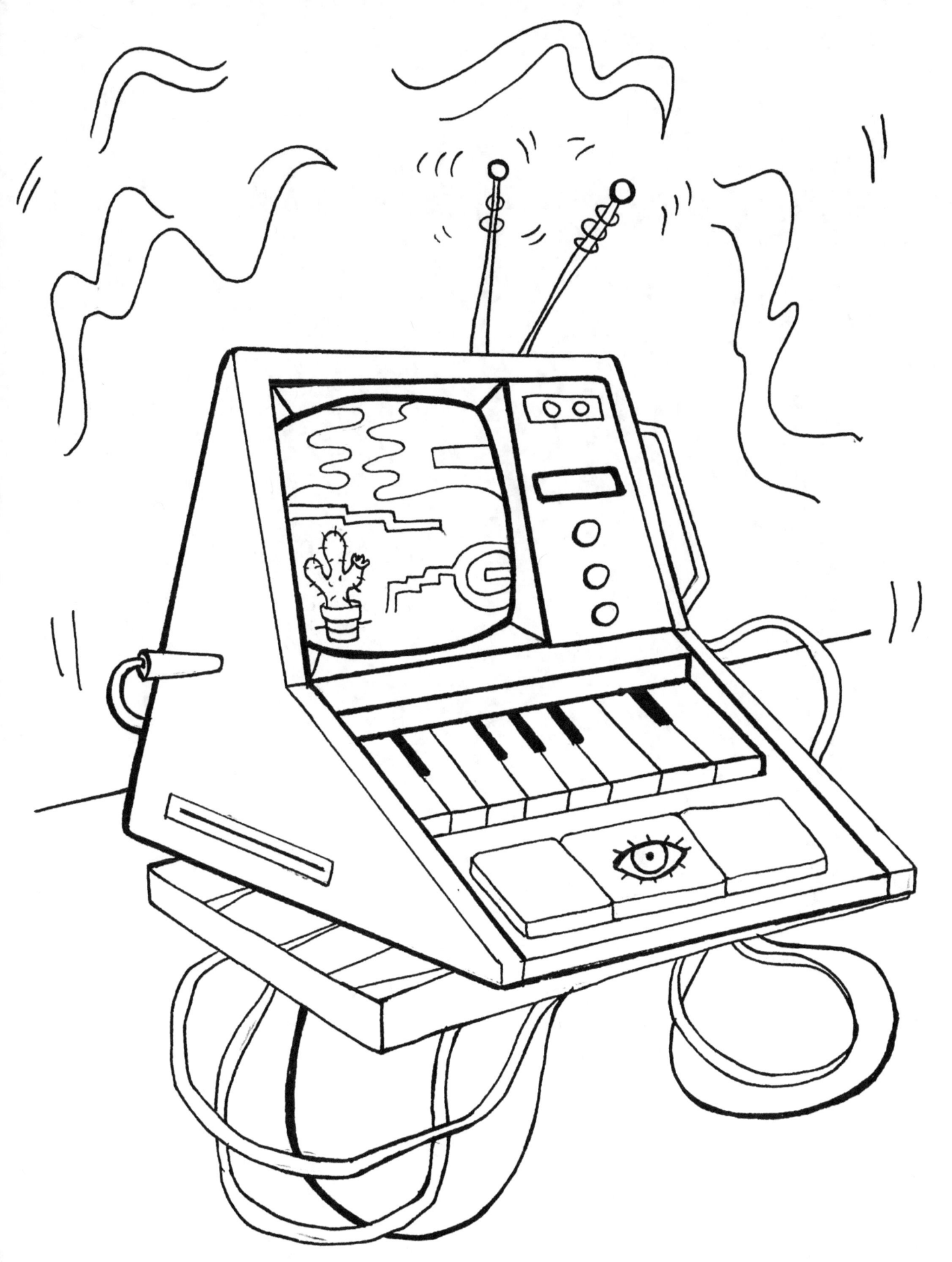

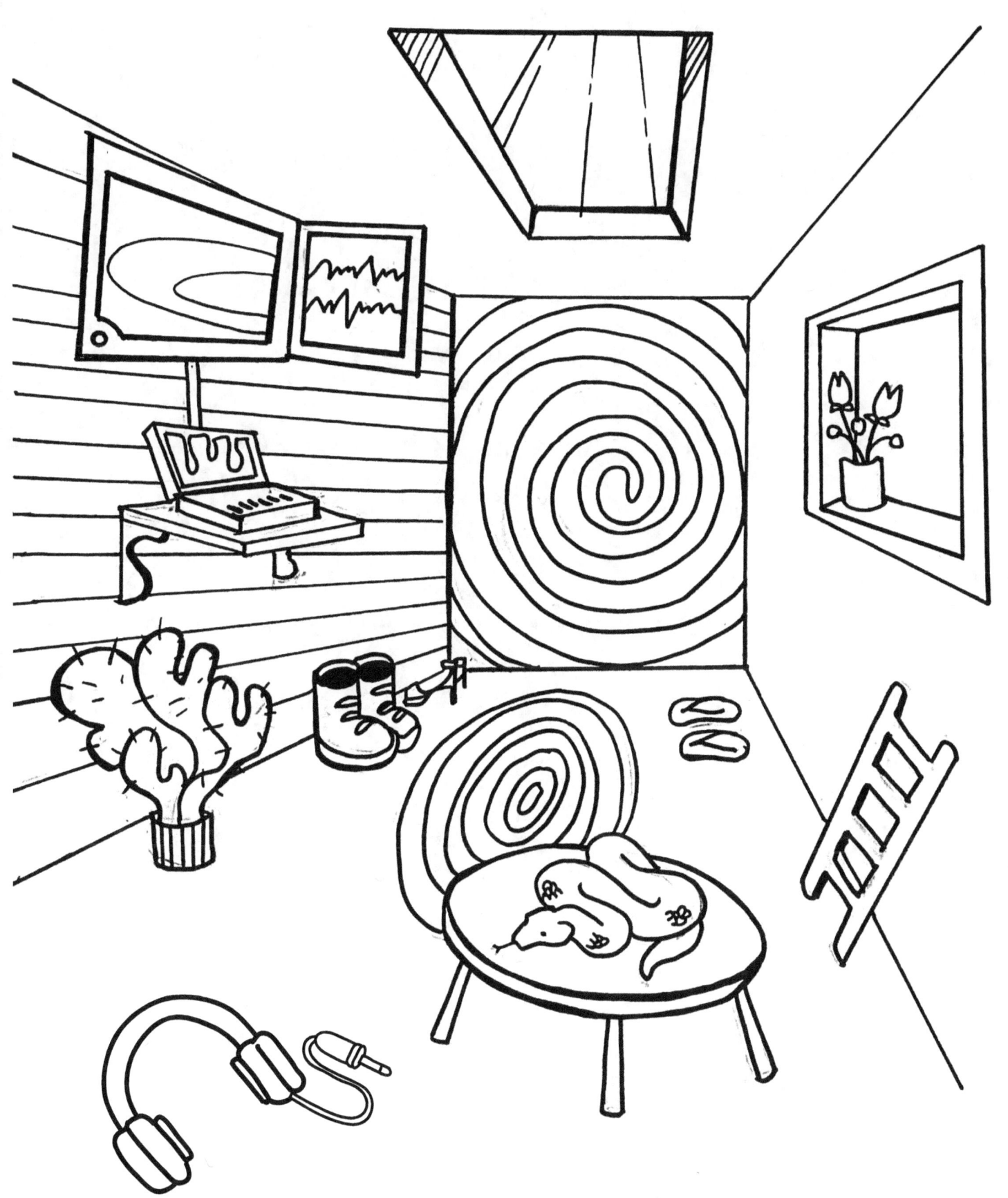

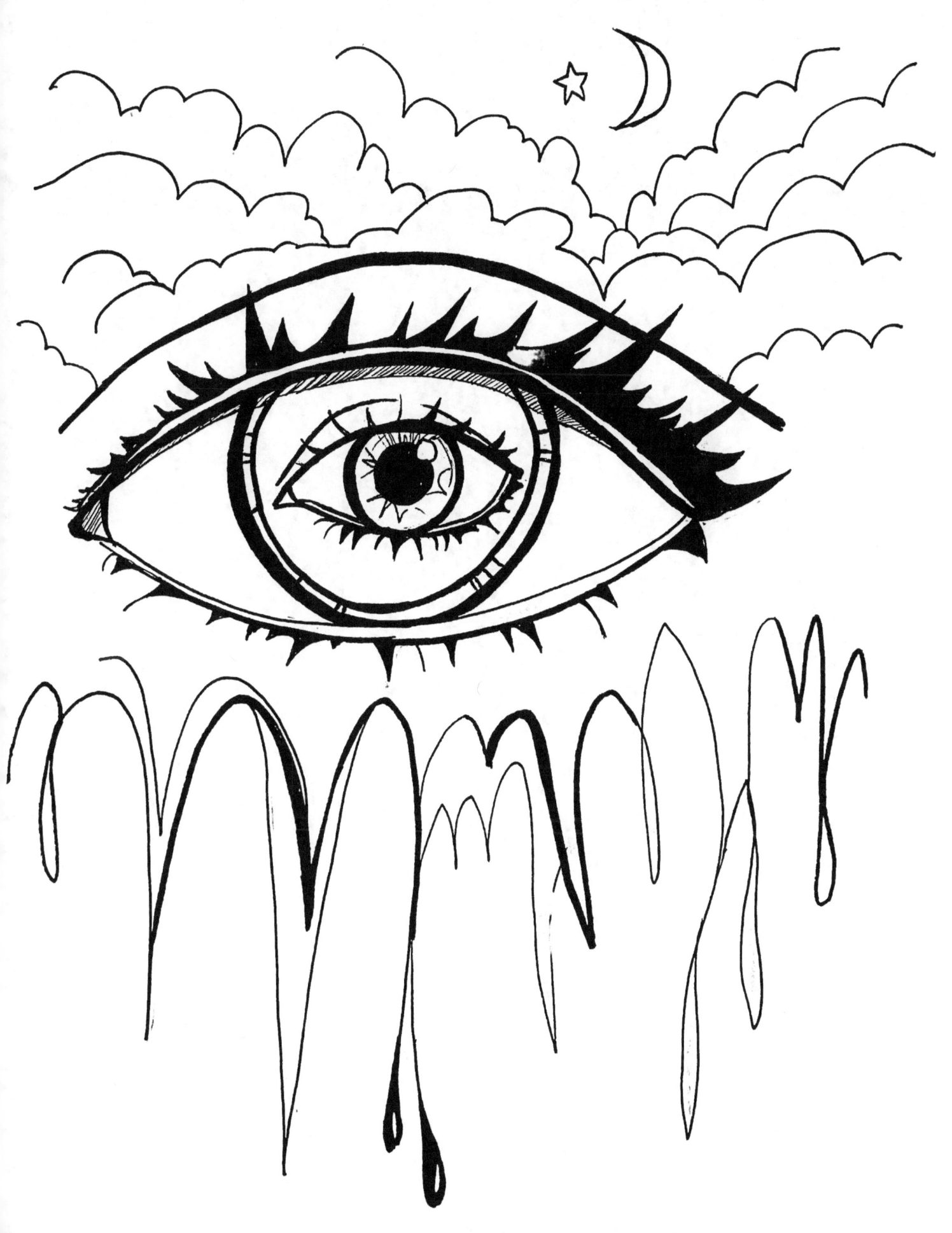

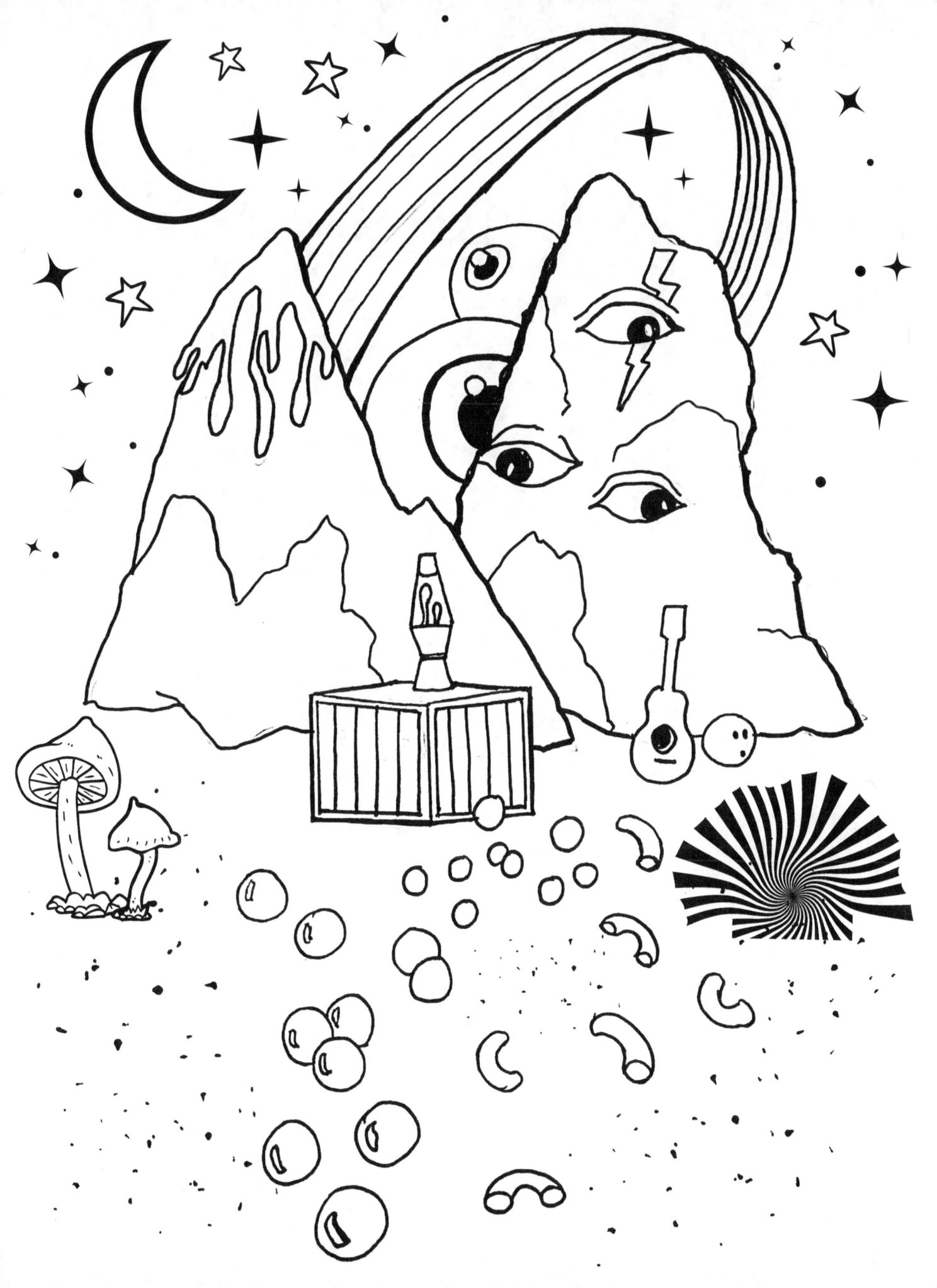

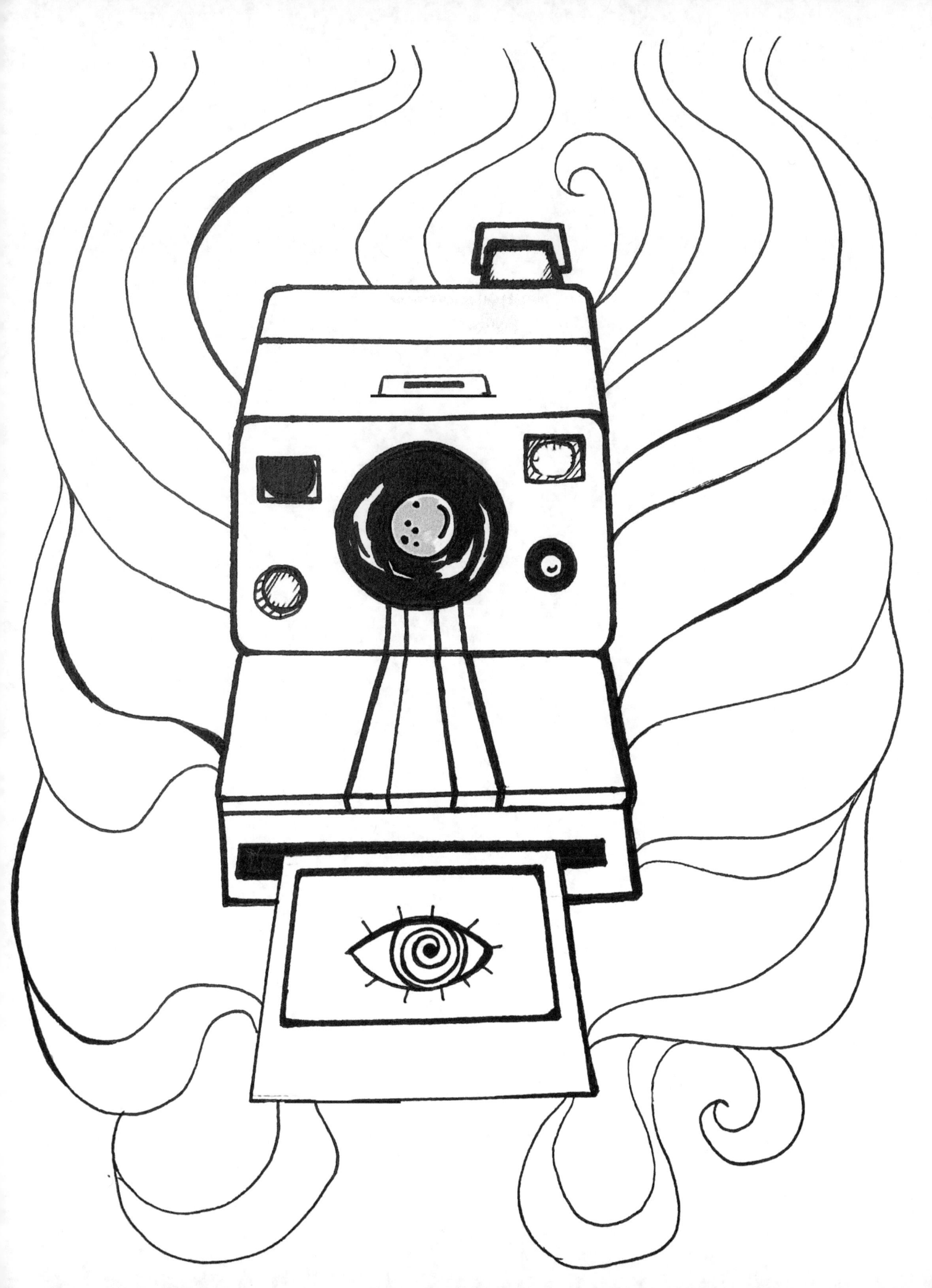

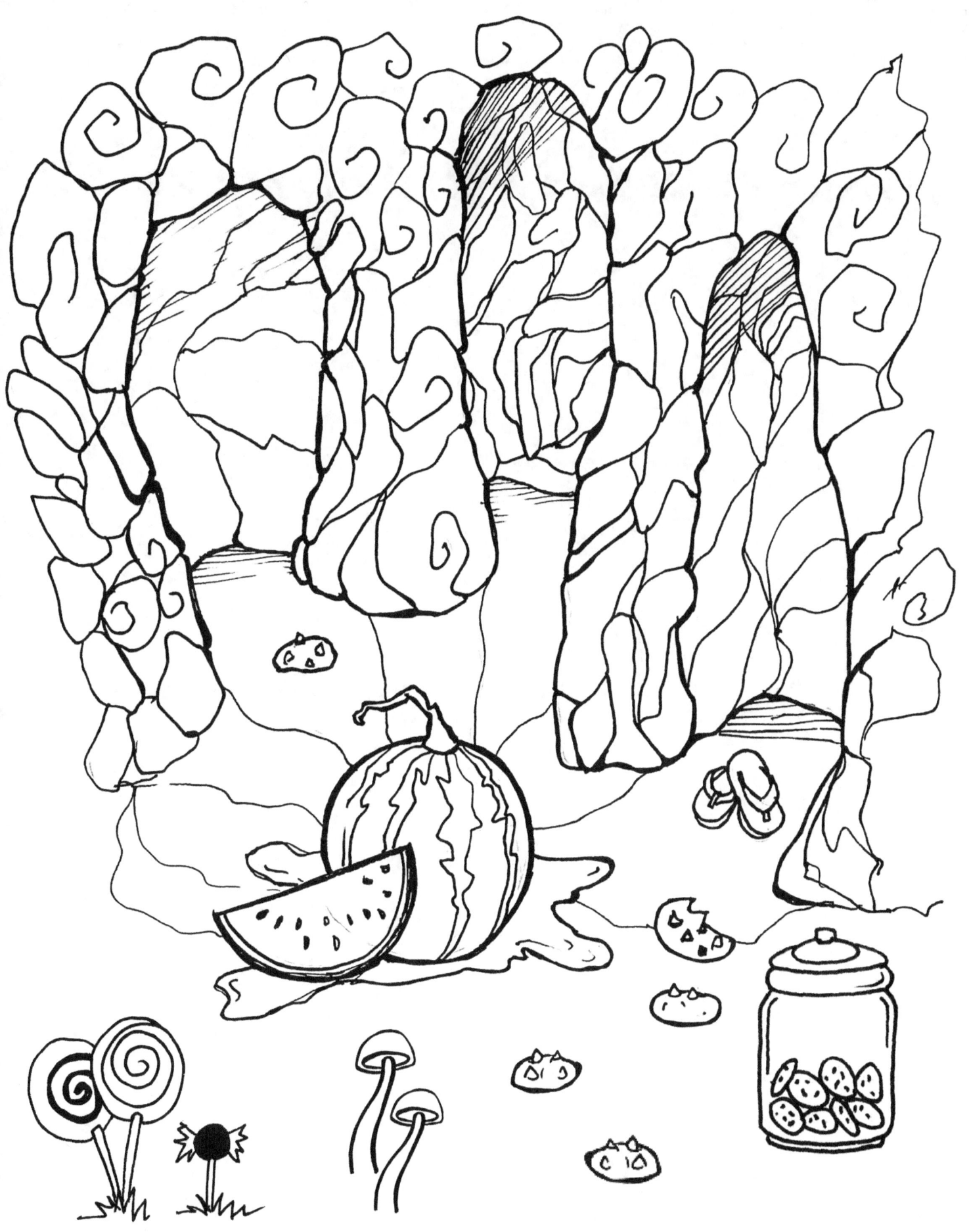

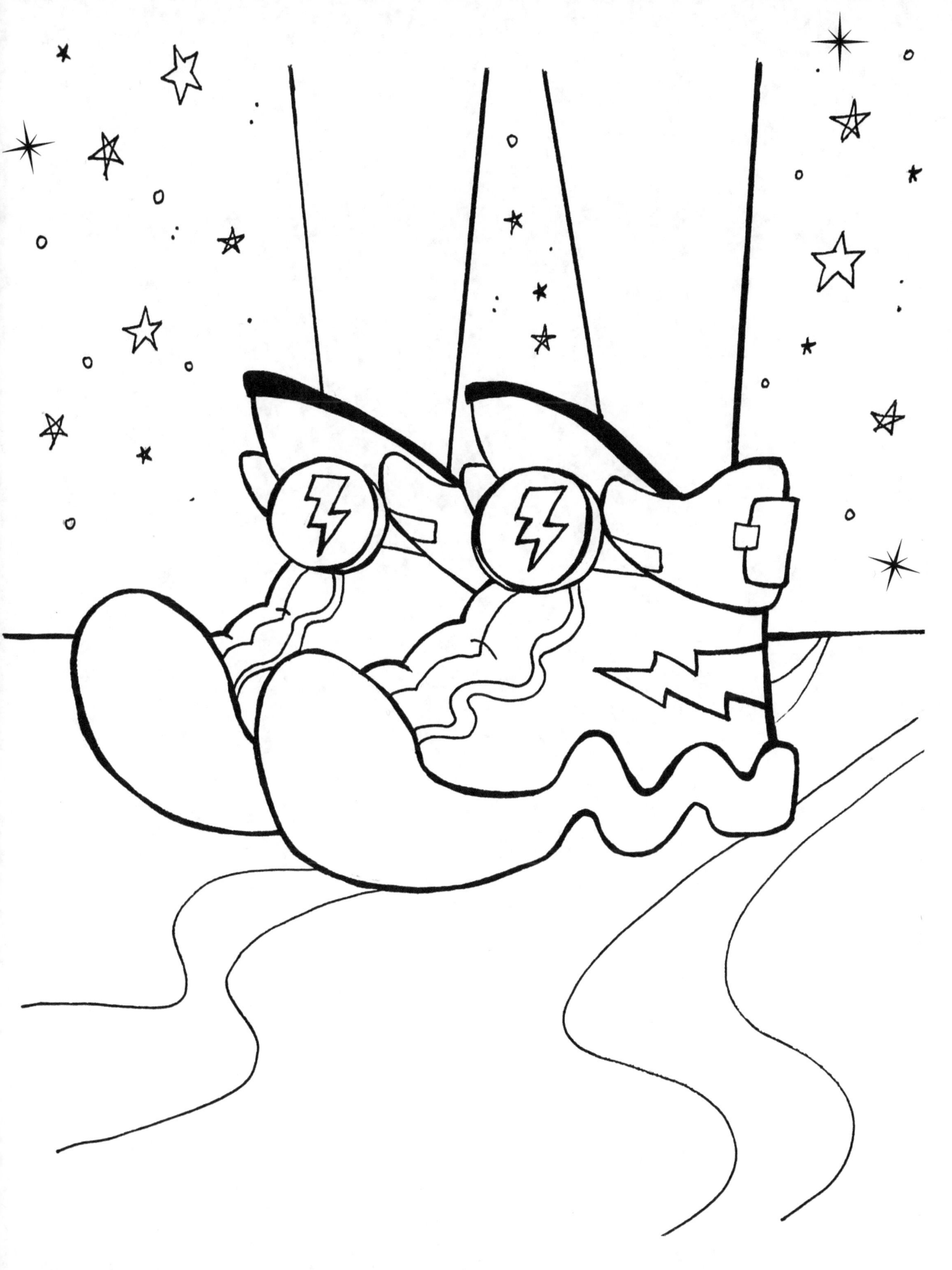

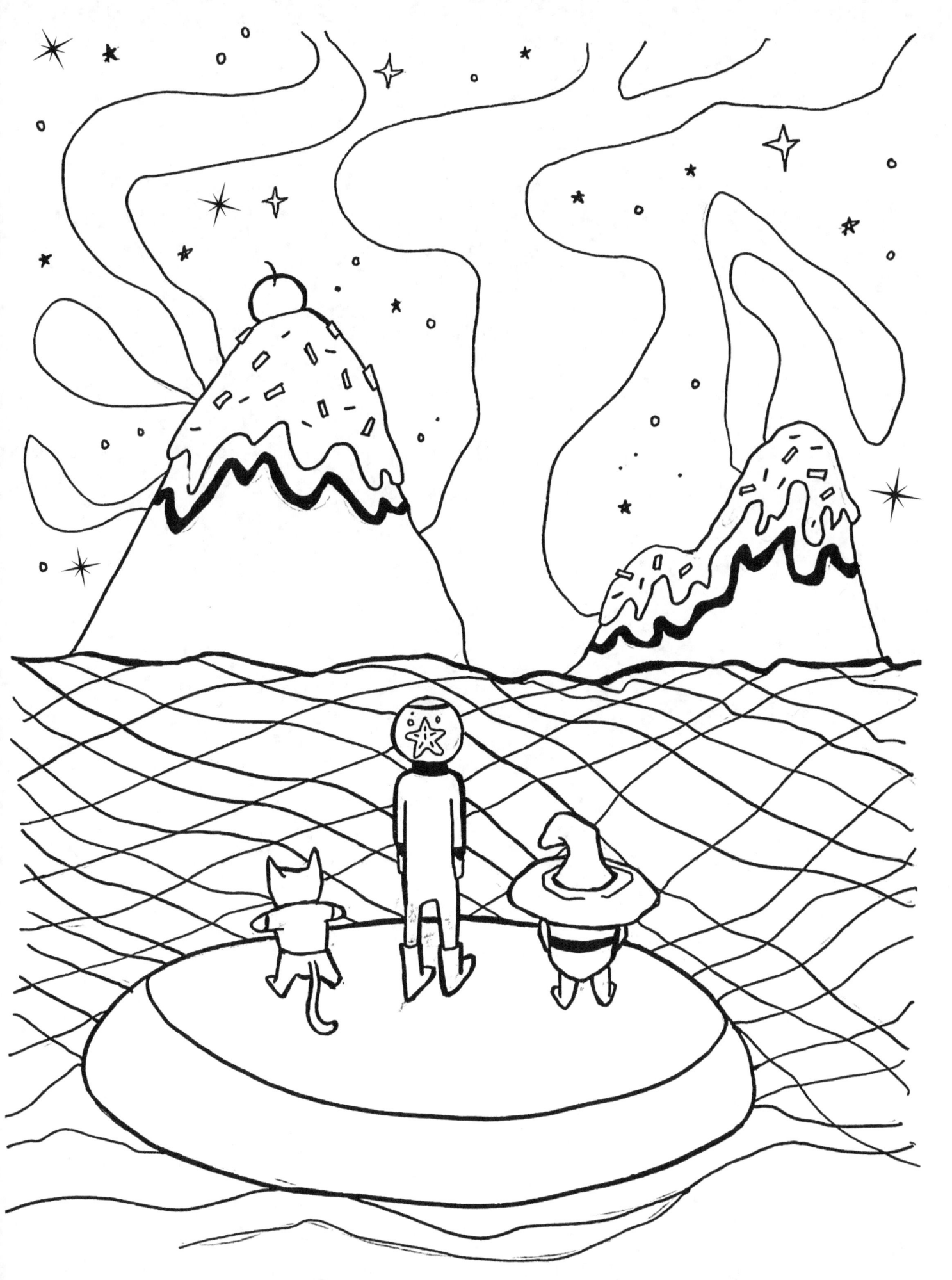

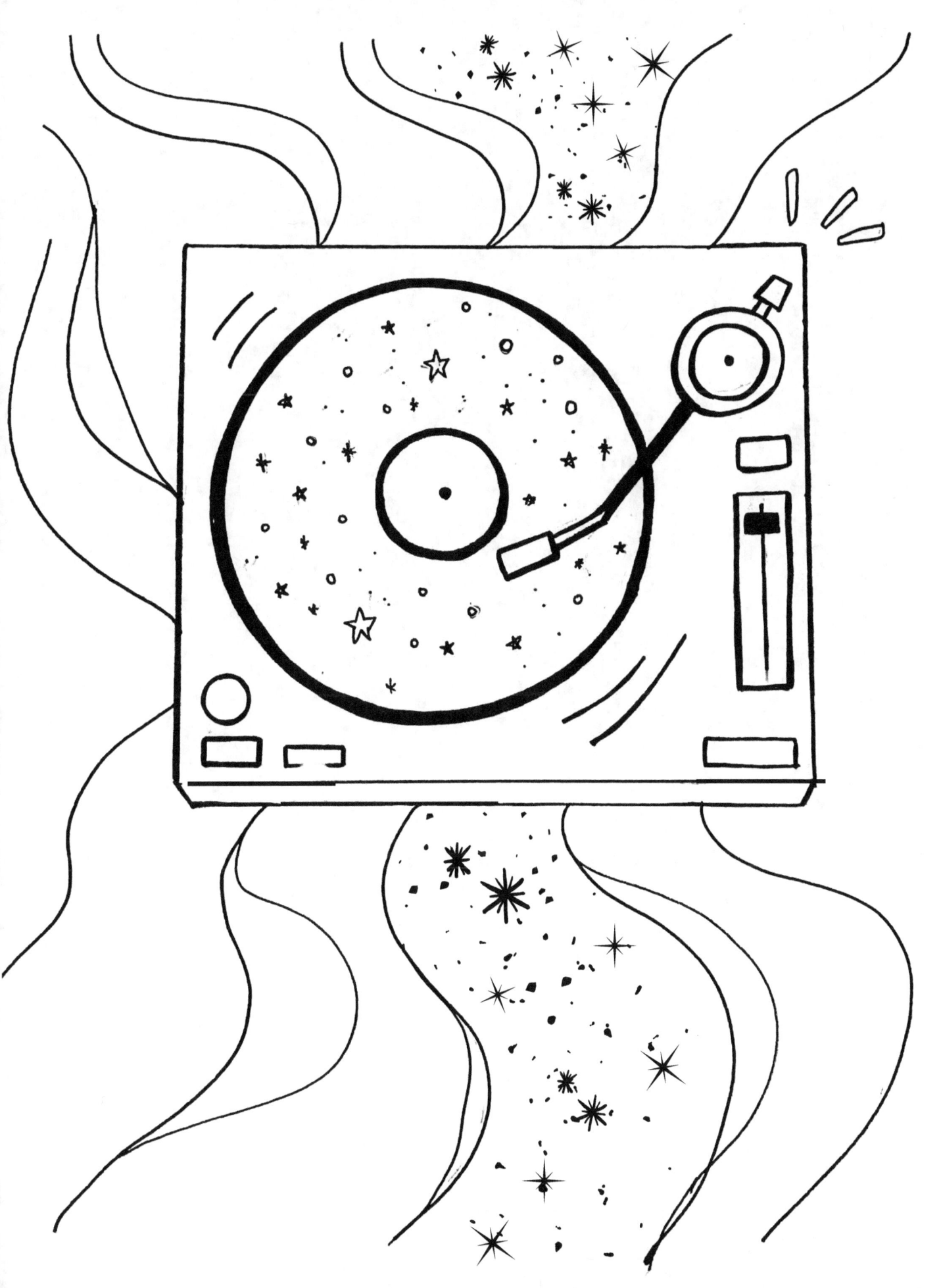

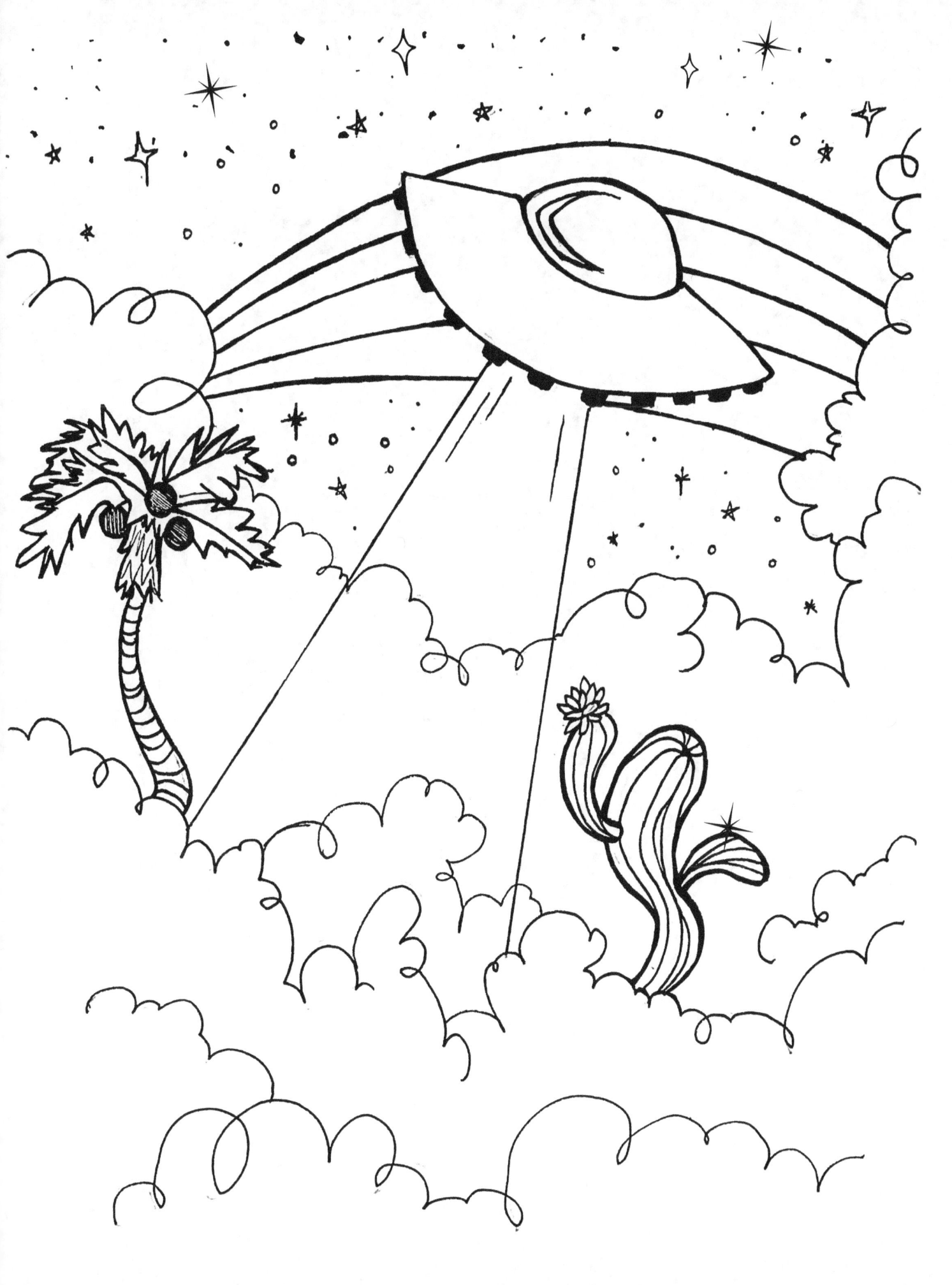

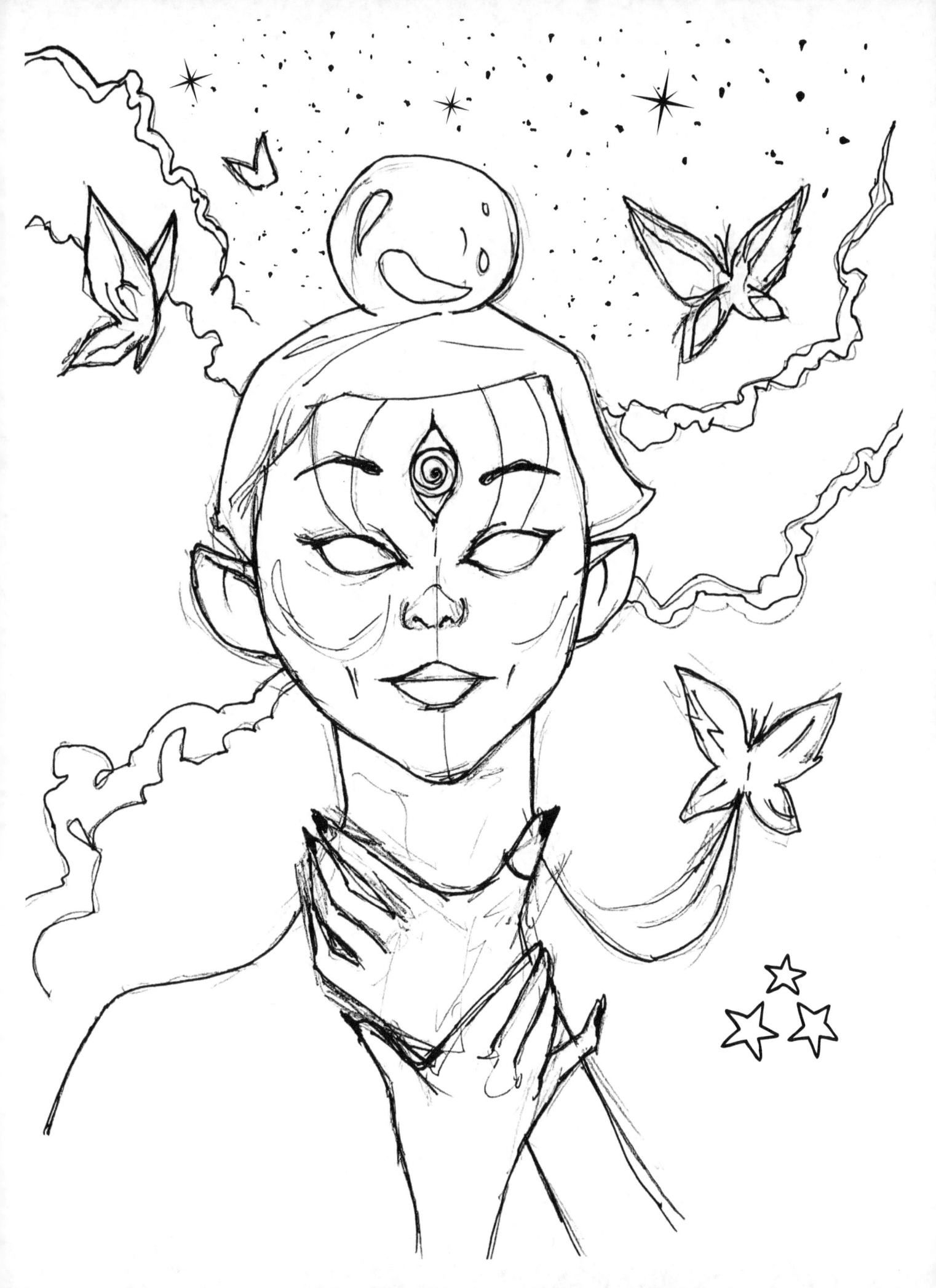

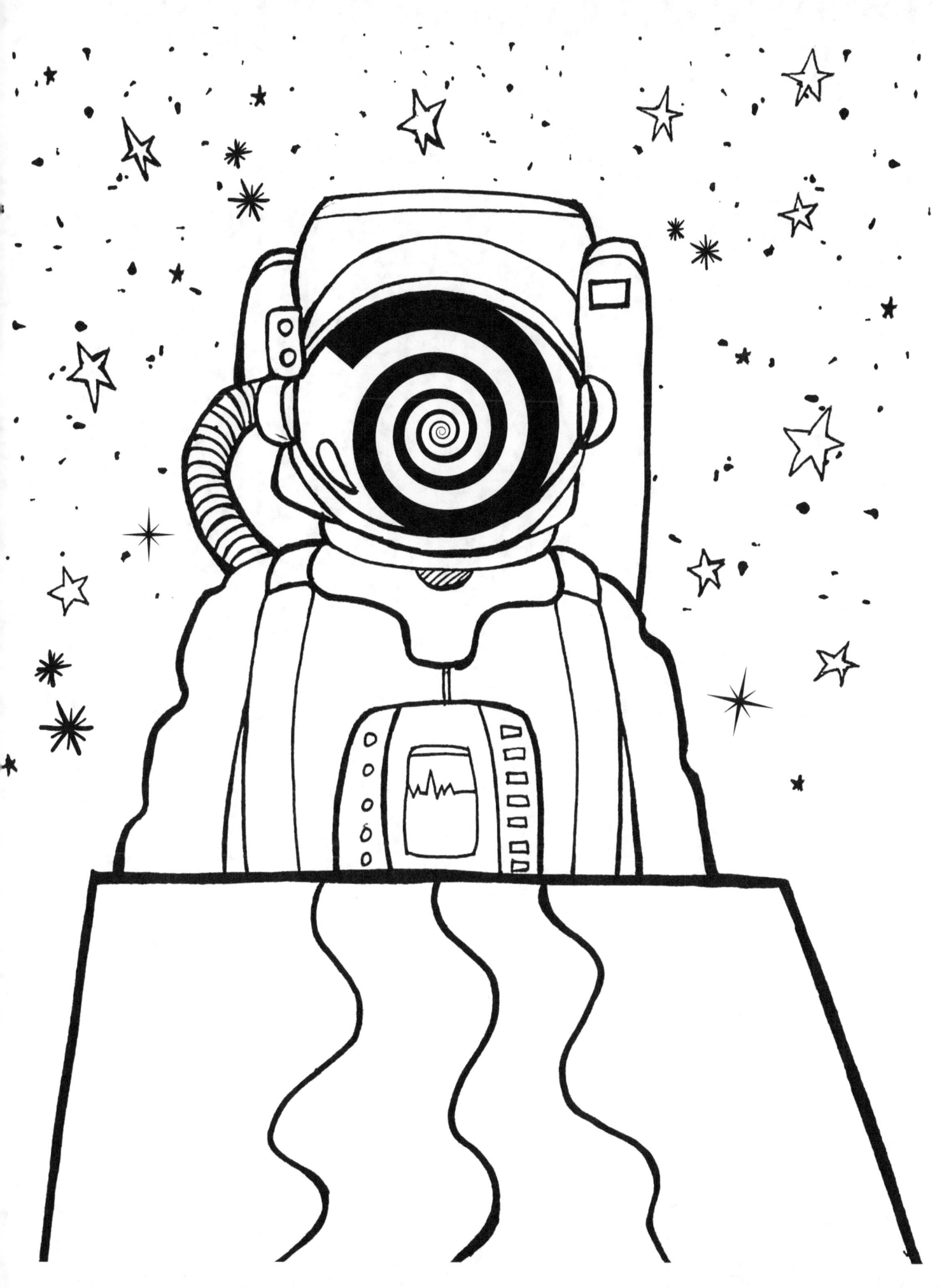

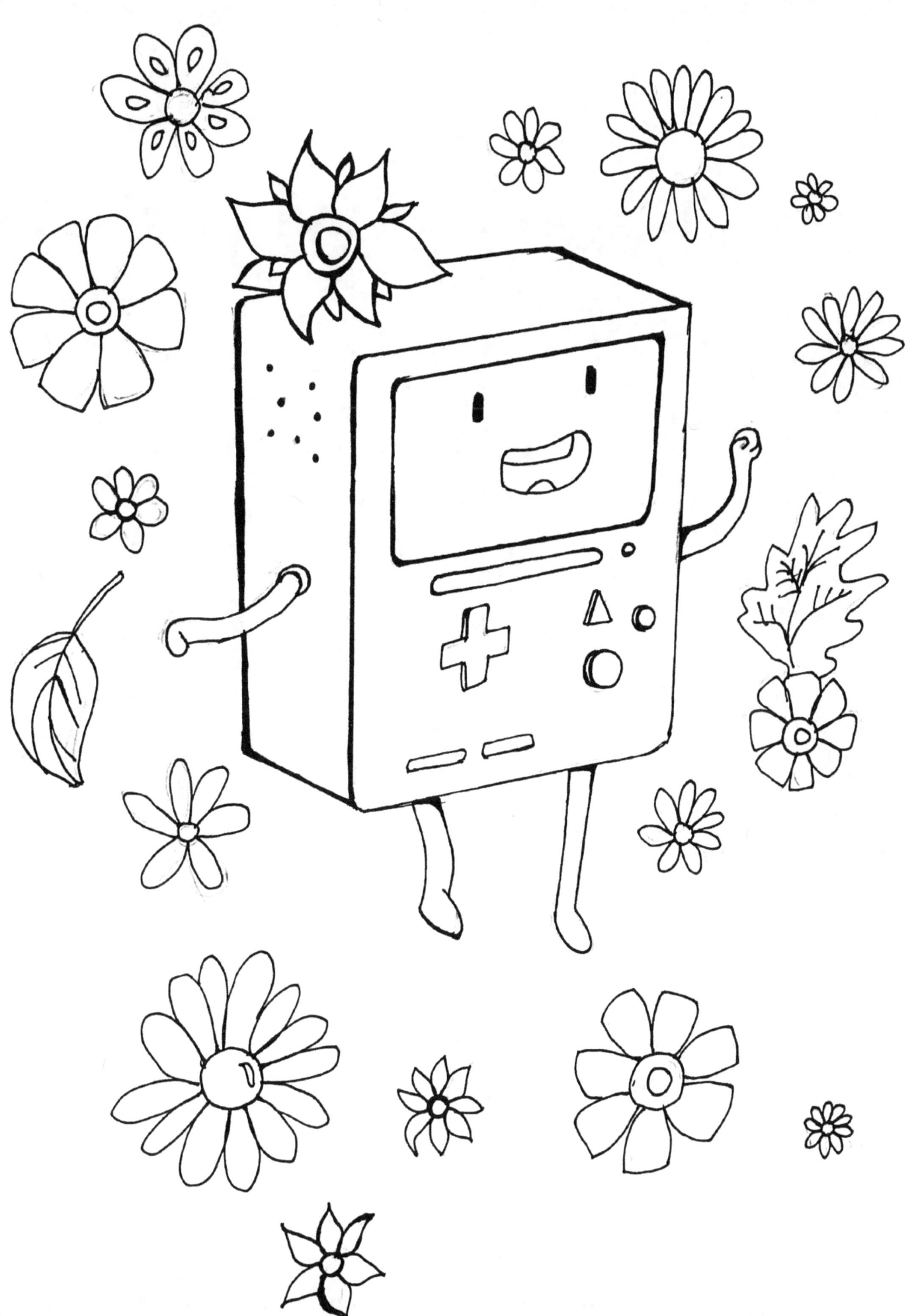

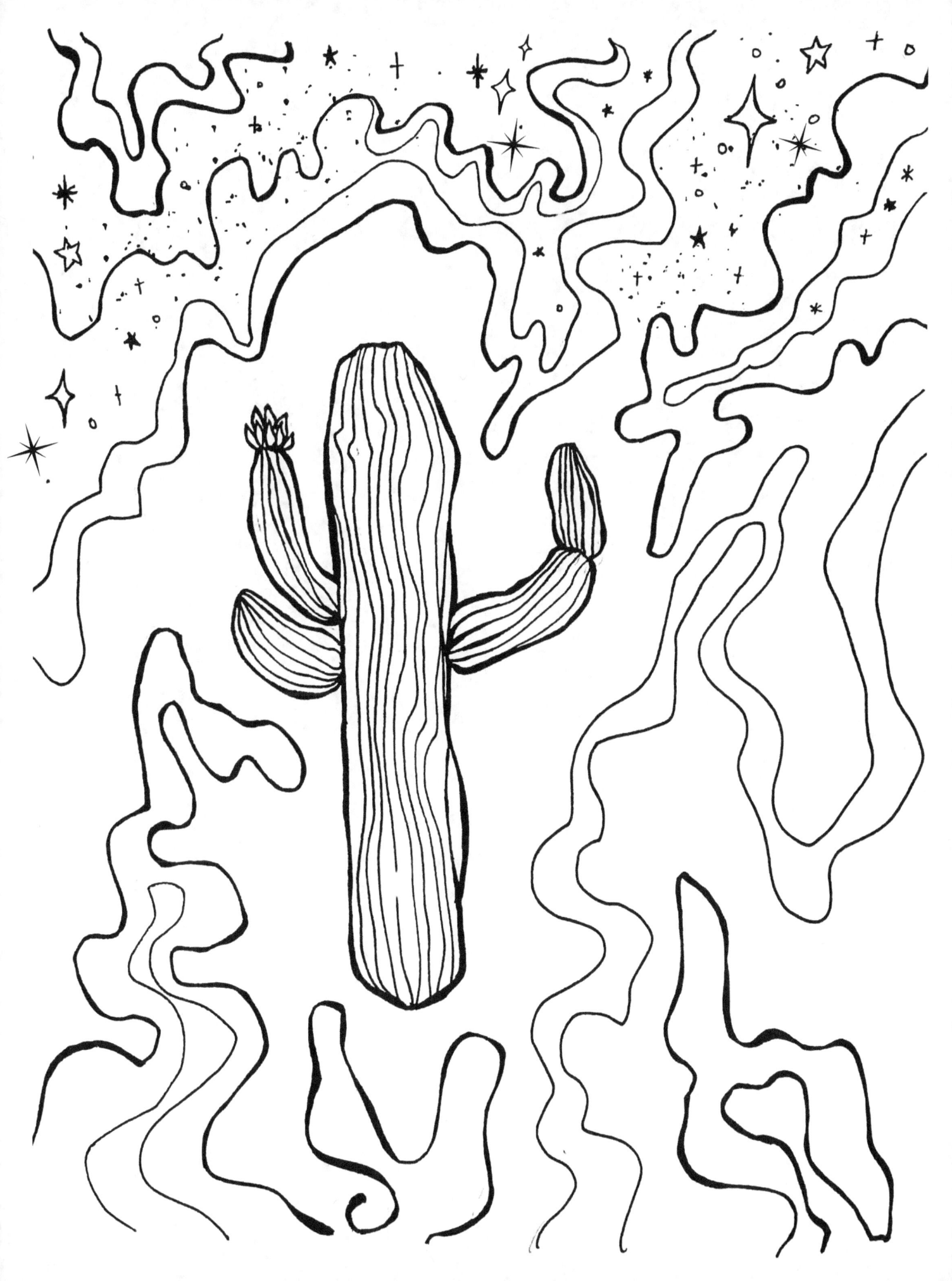

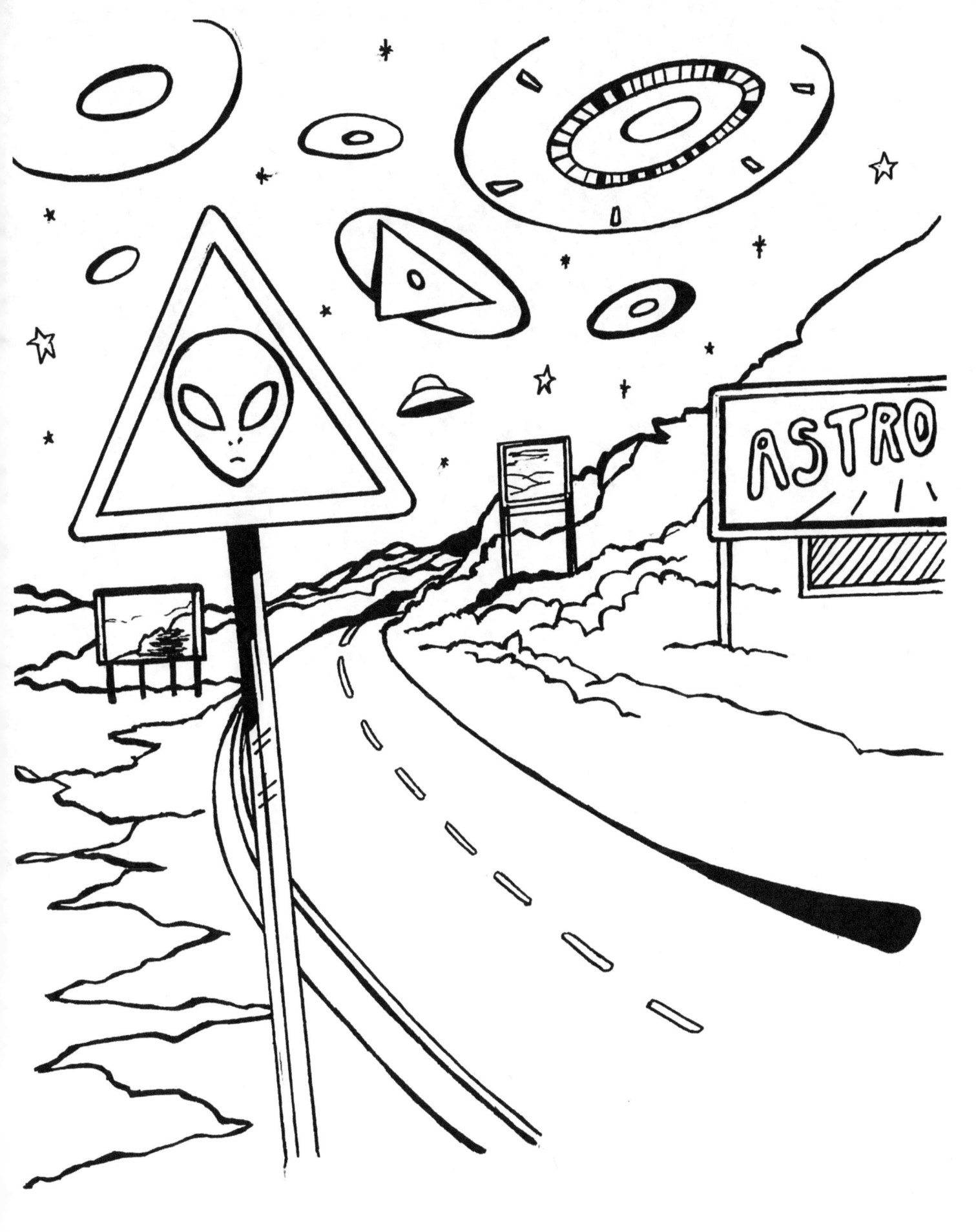

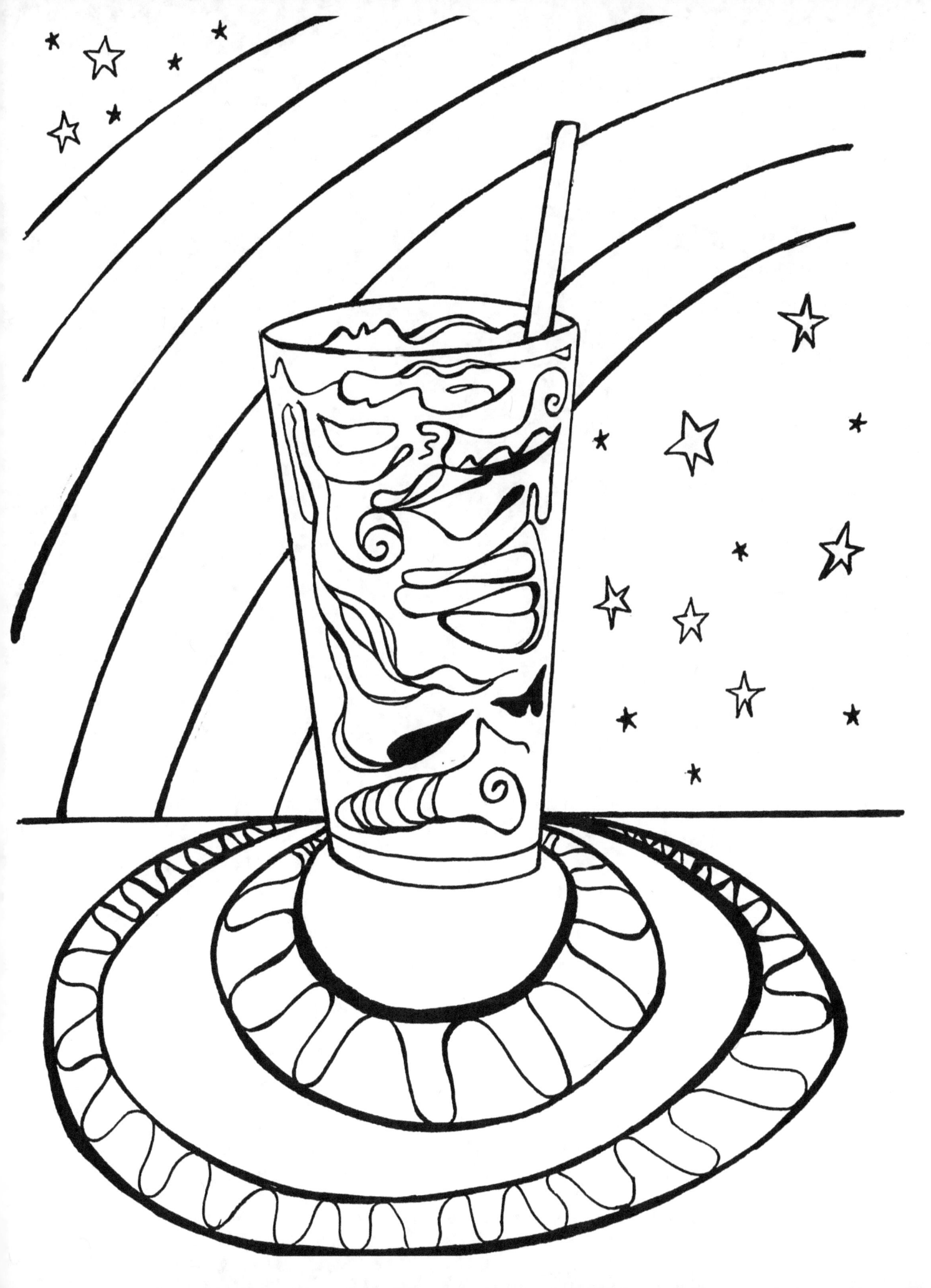

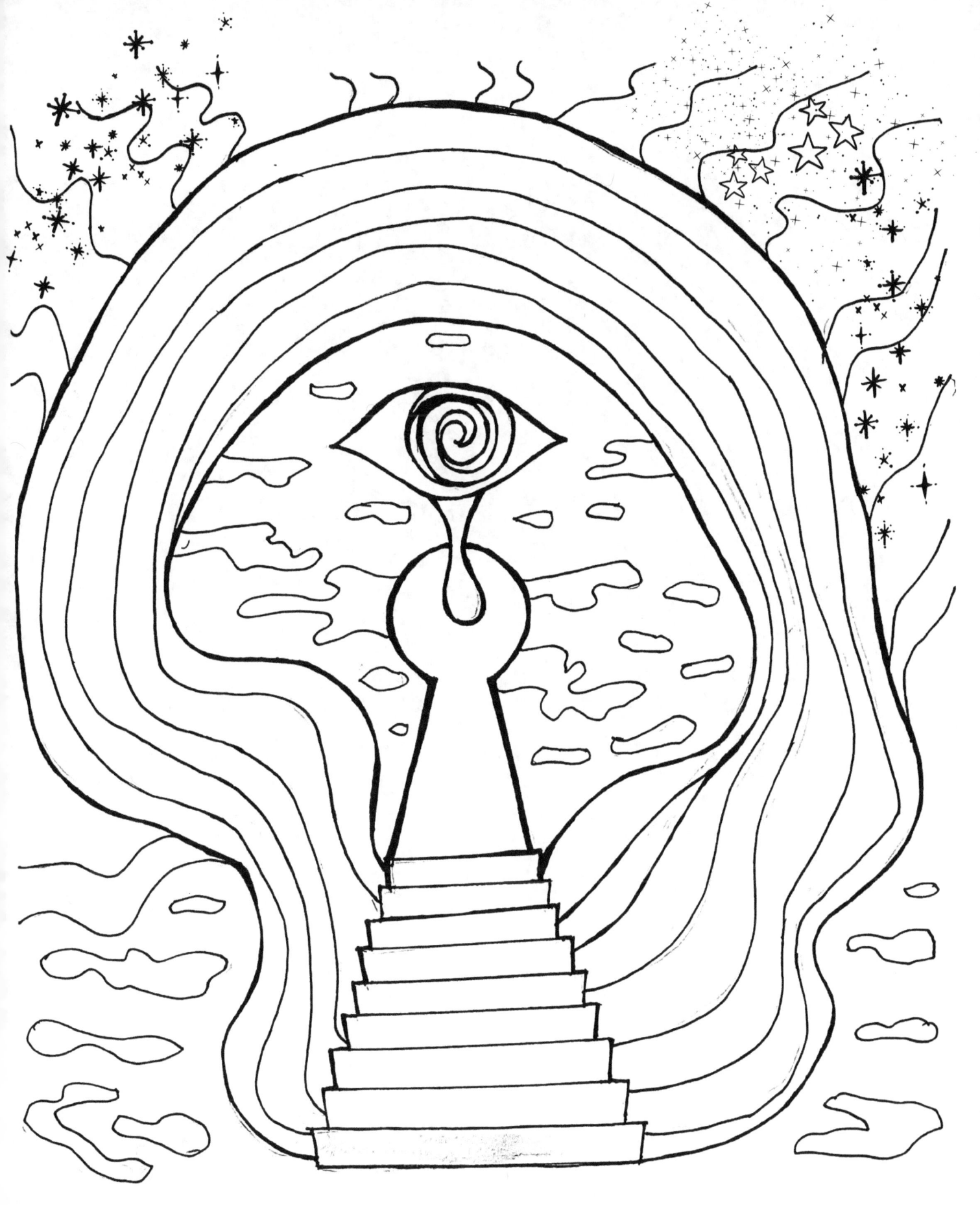

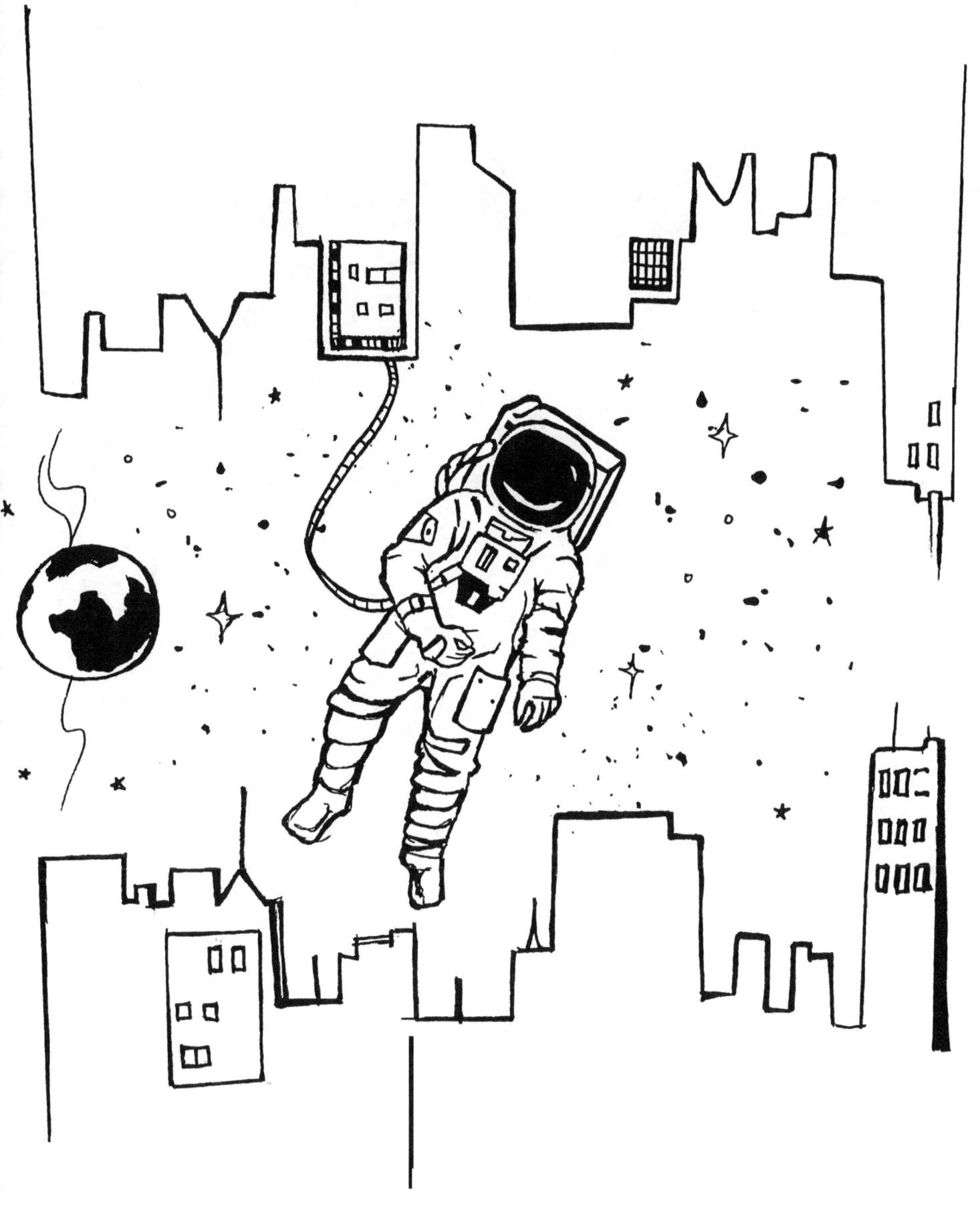

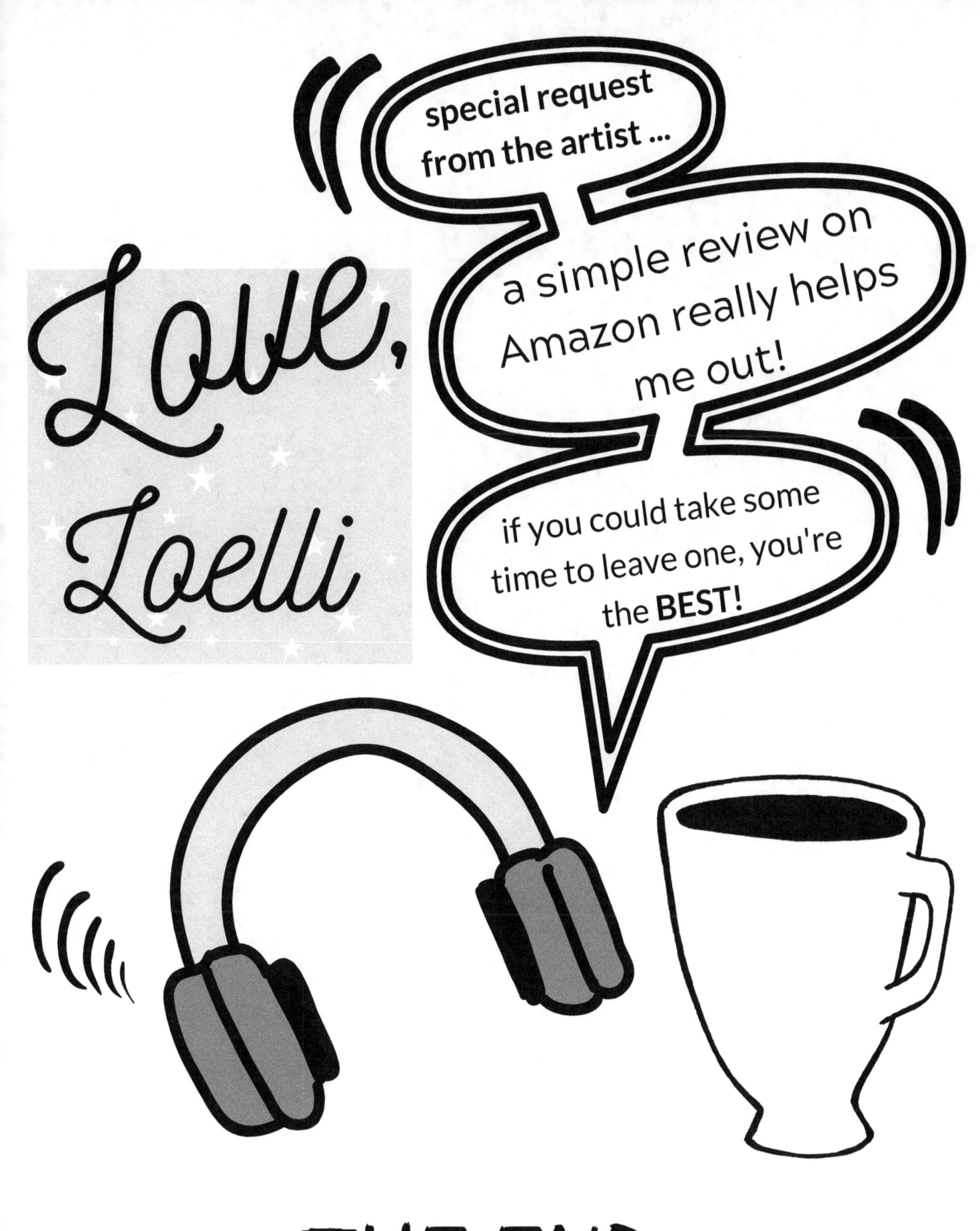